"Everyone should read this book. Mary Lenaburg is so funny and real and her words will break your heart open in the best possible way. Through her beautifully conveyed stories, she reminds us that pain will always be a part of living but that love always wins."

Jennifer Fulwiler
SiriusXM radio host and author of *Something Other Than God*

"Mary Lenaburg is such a good storyteller that you will be tempted to race through the chapters just to find out what happened next—but you'd be cheating yourself. *Be Brave in the Scared* was written for your sake to give you a step-by-tiny-step pathway to trust in God through the storms and struggles, betrayals and failures that can overwhelm anyone. Gently, Lenaburg opens the way for readers to begin to name their own personal challenges and lay them before a tender and almighty Father."

Sr. Anne Flanagan, F.S.P.
Catholic author, blogger, and speaker

"A fierce and authentic disciple of Christ, Mary Lenaburg is a truth-seeker and a truth-speaker who shares her story with a vulnerability that took my breath away. In *Be Brave in the Scared*, Lenaburg offers the deepest parts of her heart to inspire, challenge, and change you. If you find yourself struggling to see God or you desire a real and true relationship with him, read this book and be changed."

Kathryn Whitaker
Catholic blogger and author of *Live Big, Love Bigger*

"Mary Lenaburg is beloved for her warmth and her wit. She brings both to this book, tackling really tough topics with a clear-eyed look at sin and suffering. Lenaburg shines hope and grace into the dark places, and she offers tangible support and encouragement to those who find themselves there. Readers of this book will turn and face their own hard challenges with a sense that they can, indeed, be both brave enough and strong enough to keep step with God."

Elizabeth Foss
Founder of Take Up and Read and
coauthor of *Small Steps for Catholic Moms*

"Powerful, profound, and deeply moving, Mary Lenaburg's first book offers readers a front-row seat on her family's journey from brokenness, loss, and grief to healing, redemption, and joy. For anyone who has ever struggled with trusting God's plan, *Be Brave in the Scared* will leave you feeling hopeful and encouraged in your faith. I couldn't put it down; a must-read!"

Heather Renshaw
Catholic speaker and author

"Anyone who knows Mary Lenaburg knows that she is a force. She is tender and fierce, vulnerable and brave, compassionate and wise, and she has poured all of those qualities into this book. If ever you've found yourself, amid the challenges of life, struggling to breathe, find hope, or see the face of God, *Be Brave in the Scared* is for you."

Hallie Lord
SiriusXM radio host and author of *On the Other Side of Fear*

BE BRAVE IN THE SCARED

HOW I LEARNED TO TRUST GOD DURING THE MOST DIFFICULT DAYS OF MY LIFE

MARY E. LENABURG

Ave Maria Press AVE Notre Dame, Indiana

© 2019 by Mary E. Lenaburg

All rights reserved. No part of this book may be used or reproduced in any manner whatsoever, except in the case of reprints in the context of reviews, without written permission from Ave Maria Press®, Inc., P.O. Box 428, Notre Dame, IN 46556, 1-800-282-1865.

Founded in 1865, Ave Maria Press is a ministry of the United States Province of Holy Cross.

www.avemariapress.com

Paperback: ISBN-13 978-1-59471-883-0

E-book: ISBN-13 978-1-59471-884-7

Cover image © heyengel/iStock.

Cover and text design by Brianna Dombo.

Printed and bound in the United States of America.

Library of Congress Cataloging-in-Publication Data
Names: Lenaburg, Mary (Mary E.), author.
Title: Be brave in the scared : how I learned to trust God during the most difficult days of my life / Mary E. Lenaburg.
Description: Notre Dame, Indiana : Ave Maria Press, [2019] | Includes bibliographical references and index.
Identifiers: LCCN 2018056774 (print) | LCCN 2019005097 (ebook) | ISBN 9781594718847 (ebook) | ISBN 9781594718830 (pbk. : alk. paper)
Subjects: LCSH: Lenaburg, Mary (Mary E.) | Catholic women--United States--Biography. | Parents of children with disabilities--United States--Biography.
Classification: LCC BX4705.L53725 (ebook) | LCC BX4705.L53725 A3 2019 (print) | DDC 248.8/6--dc23
LC record available at https://lccn.loc.gov/2018056774.

TO JONATHAN DOUGLAS AND COURTNEY ELIZABETH:

Thank you for teaching me how to love without condition. It has been the greatest honor of my life to be your mother.

TO MY BELOVED JERRY DON:

I am never lost with you by my side. Even with all we have been through, I would say yes over and over again.

Love, thy name is Lenaburg.

CONTENTS

WELL, *THAT* DIDN'T GO AS PLANNED:

A NOTE FROM JERRY LENABURG

My wife, Mary, is a force of nature. Someone once told us that if we were characters in *Winnie-the-Pooh*, she would be Tigger and I would be Eeyore. We laughed; then we thought about it and laughed even harder. Yes, it was definitely true. My wife bounces through life with a boundless enthusiasm for helping other people and trying to put my tail back on. And my tail falls off. A lot. Thanks for noticing me.

In *Be Brave in the Scared*, you will not find a story about frolicking with puppies and unicorns (as if) and chasing rainbows to pots of gold (although that would be nice). Instead, you will read a true tale of desperation, fear, longing, doubt—and faith. Mary and I are not perfect people. We have hurt each other deeply as we struggled to come to terms with past disappointments, unmet expectations, and the fear of rejection and of not being loved for who we are.

Now, if you think that synopsis sounds a bit contradictory to Mary's Tigger persona, you're right. But here you will also read a tale of God's redeeming love for both of us, our marriage, and our family. God brought us hope, love, joy, and forgiveness when we finally stopped being knuckleheads and began to surrender, to accept his plan for our lives. Yes, we are both stubborn people. But even stubborn people can be taught eventually, if we learn to listen to God's gentle whisper. Or his spiritual two-by-four upside the head. Whichever works in a given situation.

Mary and I have been married more than thirty years, and I thank God for every minute we've had together. Have they all been perfect? Nope, not by a long shot. What they have been is real. We've lived real hope, real love, and real acceptance that everything we experienced, the good and the bad, serves a purpose in building God's kingdom. Is it always what we want? Nope, but as the song goes, "you can't always get what you want." Sometimes, though, you might find what you need instead.

While Mary was writing _Be Brave in the Scared_, she asked me what title I would give it. I immediately responded, "_Well, That Didn't Go as Planned._" She laughed. Her response was classic Mary: "Why do you always look for life to be so predictable? The adventure we have lived is better than I have ever thought possible." That is my wife: Tigger to the max, always living her life for hope. Our daughter, Courtney, taught her that.

I hope _Be Brave in the Scared_ makes you laugh and cry. But more, I hope that reading our story will inspire you to trust in the God who loves you and wants only the best for you as you deal with all the challenges life will throw your way.

Jerry Lenaburg
September 24, 2018

INTRODUCTION

If I bet everything I had that there was no one out there who would want to trade their life story for mine, I'd win. That's because mine has been everything but a fairy tale. Honestly, who would choose to spend decades caring for a severely disabled person, have their marriage wounded by pornography, struggle with mental health, or lose a beloved child before her twenty-third birthday? If asked, most people would check "none of the above" on that question. Somehow, I ended up checking "all of the above."

Overwhelming? You have no idea. Exhausting? I can't tell you how often I just wanted to go to sleep and stay asleep. The funny thing, though, is that I'm pretty sure I wouldn't want to trade my life's experiences for anyone else's—not even for the "normal life" I thought I wanted (you know, the one I used to think was unfairly taken from me). Why? Because the circumstances of my life, as challenging as they have been, have taught me how to trust God—as in trust him completely with every single aspect of my life.

Once you learn to trust God on the most difficult days of your life, every day has meaning. Life isn't all flowers and chocolates, but it isn't empty or senselessly cruel either. Surrender to God's will, it turns out, is surrender to love. It took me years to learn that, and I learned it only because I was blessed with a gifted teacher: my daughter, Courtney. Whether you share some of the challenges I've faced or not, I'm sure you have a teacher in your life too.

I have told our family's story to audiences all over the country. My hope is that this book will help you see the beauty and grace in *your* story. At the end of each chapter, I have included a related scripture verse and a blank journaling page just for you. Draw, write, whatever. Use these pages to think, shout, or pray. God is listening.

You don't need to worry about the challenges in your life. We all have them, we all make our way through them, and we all create them for the people closest to us. What you need to do is stop holding your breath and trust God. He may not take your suffering away, but he will teach you how to be brave in the scared, just the way he—and Courtney—taught me.

CHAPTER ONE

OUT OF CONTROL

Control is power. When we have a plan, we can tell ourselves that we are in charge of our lives. It's easy to be brave. We feel confident when we know what to expect. After all, things are locked down. Expectations are met. Everything is bright and shiny. But control is a funny thing. One minute unicorns roam the world, flowers fall from the sky, and cupcakes don't have calories. The next minute a thundering herd of rhinos trample all our delusions, and we are left vulnerable and afraid.

To be in control means believing you're directing your path and making the right choices. That's why many of us are, well, controlling. The best part of being a control freak? Everyone around you respects you and your decisions. They buy into the illusion that your life actually is the Pinterest board it looks like, and they eat your cupcakes without gaining a pound, because they believe you have control.

Isn't this the ideal we yearn for? Control over every aspect of our lives—our health, finances, kids, and marriages? Nothing bad would ever happen because we simply wouldn't allow it.

REALITY CHECK

But that isn't real life. Reality hits us when we pull out our daily planners full of careful lists and then are honestly surprised when we can't cross anything off before we go to bed. We expect events to happen in our lives at a certain time and to unfold in a certain way that is predetermined by us. And when things don't happen that way—when we discover that the cupcakes have five hundred calories each—we just might feel as if we're twirling around naked in the middle of the street, screaming at the sky for an explanation.

The fact is that most of us get up every morning with the notion that we are basically in control. Then, on one of those mornings, something happens that shows us we never were. And if we're among those who hold the ideal of control in a death grip, an encounter with reality can leave us lonely, curled up, and crying in a corner (hopefully not in a dirty bathrobe, clutching a bottle of bourbon, and tearing into a bag of chips).

While we're in this self-pity-induced haze, we can't see clearly. The illusion of control steals our joy. Why? you may ask. Because this thief brings along with it two sidekicks known as expectations and comparison. Life brings you situations that are not what you wanted or expected, and it doesn't necessarily bring you what it brings to others. It's like when you order a big, juicy bacon cheeseburger and bite into it, only to discover that someone has substituted turkey bacon and tofu. Meanwhile, the friend you're having lunch with gets exactly what she ordered specifically the way she wanted it. It's just not fair.

Great expectations. We all have them, don't we? I know I did! I planned to get married in my twenties and start a family. I assumed, with extreme confidence, that my future husband and I would picket-fence our lives. We'd buy a charming house in a darling neighborhood and send our genius kids to private school. The kids would be incredibly smart, motivated, and very holy, and our marital relationship would put the greatest love stories to shame.

No, I wasn't a spoiled brat with a big entitlement problem. I just wanted the soaps to be real, except that Frisco would choose me over Felicia. Needless to say, I never met Frisco, and Port Charles was far from my reality. When my expectations were not met, I wasn't angry, just confused—I didn't understand why my plans weren't coming together. But I was still determined to eat the calorie-free cupcake, so I kept on making plans and building expectations and forging ahead. It wasn't until I was married with two children that life's hard truths began to chip away at my allegiance to control.

I guess, in a way, I'm lucky that things fell apart when I was younger, while I could still stay up past ten p.m. and get up at six a.m. without the urge to wear yoga pants all day. Since then, it's taken me a quarter century to come to a place of realistic self-awareness and reliance on the One who truly controls things. But it's not yet time to talk about God. Right now, this story is about me. (It's okay. He and I have chatted about this, and he's okay with it. He knows it's going to be all about him anyway.)

Let's get to the real story. Once upon a time, my husband, Jerry, and I were living out his dream to be a naval aviator. Although it meant long months apart, I happily followed him from duty station to duty station. It was a great adventure where he was the captain and I his first mate. We were a team with a plan. And a plan meant we were in control—until we weren't.

AT THE FONT

"I baptize you in the name of the Father, and of the Son, and of the Holy Spirit," the priest said. "Amen." For Christians, these holy words bring new life. On a crisp Sunday afternoon in September 1992, my non-Catholic husband; three-year-old son, Jonathan; and I stood around the font in the suburban Maryland church that I grew up in as a priest spoke these words over, baptized, and anointed our one-month-old daughter, Courtney Elizabeth.

While the priest did his thing, I made lists in my mental daily planner. I hate to admit it, but this was a get-this-kid-baptized-quickly kind of ceremony. We had a few of my large extended family in attendance, but despite the fact that she wore the family baptismal gown, there would be no party. After the ceremony we were heading back to Maine. Why? Because the following week, the navy was moving us from Maine to Washington, DC. We had a schedule to keep, and there was no room for deviation. That came back to bite me in a big way.

Just as the priest poured holy water over our daughter's head, Courtney arched her back, and her face turned purple. She held her breath and her body jerked once, twice, and a third time. Her movements were so sudden that I almost dropped her. Then she turned into a spaghetti noodle, and I pulled her in close. *What was happening? Was the water too cold? Was it too loud in the church? What was going on?* I glanced at my father and then my husband. Had they seen that? My father, who was fighting cancer at the time, went pale, while my husband's gaze darted around the church like a sniper's on the hunt. My breath caught, and my vision blurred. Something *had* happened. Something was wrong.

POWERLESS

Within the hour, I found myself in an emergency room with our daughter actively seizing. Nurses buzzed around Courtney like bees around a sunflower. It was confusing, disorienting, and just plain scary. Minutes or hours later, a doctor gave our daughter a shot in the thigh, and she went limp in my arms. The doctor took her gently in his arms and disappeared without speaking a word. I didn't know that when he walked away with our daughter, our world would change forever.

The next few hours were hell. By the time we saw Courtney again, the sun had gone down, and the heavy weight of discontent had settled on both Jerry and me. Our tempers were short, and our fear hit the top of the charts. We wanted answers, and no one had them. We heard big, scary terms. Nurses took blood and placed an IV in our daughter's small hand, and doctors ordered an electroencephalogram (EEG) and a spinal tap. There were many tears, both Courtney's and mine.

Looking at her in the hospital crib, I couldn't get over how small she was. Courtney was just a little baby, only five weeks old. Her hand was all bandaged to keep the IV in place, and there were wires poking out from underneath a little hospital gown that had pink elephants on it. Machines hanging over her bed hummed and beeped with regularity. Every time she had a seizure, alarms rang out and an army of hospital staff came rushing into the room.

The whole thing was overwhelming, and I was losing my grip on my emotions. To make things even worse (because things can *always* get worse), it was well past Jonathan's bedtime. Jerry took our son back to my parents' house so he could leave in the morning to make it to Maine in time to meet the military movers. A terrifying realization set in: not only was I alone but I also had no control over this situation.

As they pushed Courtney's crib down the empty hall in the basement of the hospital, passing one hazardous material sign after another, I heard only silence. They wouldn't let me go back with her; once again I was relegated to the sidelines. I don't like the sidelines. I'm an all-in kind of girl. Since I couldn't participate, I paced the waiting room and prayed. All of my expectations had been doused with lighter fluid and set aflame. I wasn't happy.

And what does an unhappy Mary do? She yells at God: *Don't you dare let her die.*

Then Mary begs: *Please, don't let her die.*

And then Mary makes a deal: *I'll take her any way you wish to give her to me, just don't let her die.*

That night was the beginning of my seven-day vigil in the pediatric intensive care unit (PICU). I never left Courtney's side for one moment that week. I was too afraid something would happen while I was gone. If it had, I knew that I would never forgive myself. At the end of the week, with Courtney still seizing multiple times a day, this was all the doctors could tell me: "Ma'am? We have no idea why your daughter is having seizures." It's hard to describe the utter despair I felt in that moment. Jerry was still in Maine, my son was with my parents, and I was alone.

As the doctors apologized and promised to keep searching for answers, they handed me prescription drugs and gave me instructions on how to care for Courtney. All I could hear was my own internal shouts into an eternal silence. *God hadn't heard my screams and cries or taken me up on any of my bargains*, I thought. Once the doctors left, I fell to my knees and wept. I knew what was happening: God was punishing me.

PERFECT

I once heard it said that to have children is to allow your heart to walk outside your body. It's a vulnerable and trusting act to bring a child into the world, and Jerry and I had done that twice now. What we had not told anyone was that the week before this horrific turn of events, I'd had my tubes tied at the age of twenty-five. Despite the Church's teaching on being open to life, Jerry and I had decided that we were done having babies. There were too many variables at play—from my difficult pregnancies to his desire for a very small family—for us to take any chances. We wanted to be in control of our own destinies, and we were happy with one boy and one girl. Two perfect children for our perfect life.

But our perfect life was circling the drain, and panicked questions taunted me. Was God angry? Was he taking revenge because we had closed ourselves to the future gift of children? Was Courtney going to die?

I felt terrified and confused and betrayed. In my mind, our situation confirmed that God was a tyrant. I felt just like I had in grade school when I was sent to the principal's office for breaking a rule, except now my daughter was paying the price. There isn't a word in the dictionary to define my anger that day. All my life I had been taught that Jesus had come to save us by suffering for us on the Cross. Yet now, he was allowing Courtney to suffer. What was *that* about?

I have to be honest: at this point in my life, I thought God was a bully. I had not felt his love or experienced his mercy. I was still determined to solve the problem, to find a way to fix all of this somehow. Surrender was not an option, just a sign of weakness—and I *had* to be strong. If God wouldn't help me, I'd do it myself.

I can hear your laughter from here. Yes, I had much to learn. I got on my knees deeply angry with God. I unleashed my fear and anxiety and gave him my complete and honest opinion of the current situation. Because Jerry wasn't Catholic and had a very loose relationship with God, I felt utterly alone in this. I knew that if either of us was going to pray, it would have to be me and me alone. Luckily, God is as gracious as he is loving, and he didn't give up on me. In the midst of my silent screams, I felt a slight shift in my heart, like a hiccup of time, a moment of calm in the middle of one hell of a storm. I took a breath and God spoke words into my heart. I'll be forever grateful to the Holy Spirit for allowing me to hear them: *I love her. She belongs to me. And she's perfect just as she is.*

God saw Courtney and loved her just as she was. In the midst of the chaos and the suffering, he saw perfection and claimed our daughter for his own.

AN INVITATION

I've been a Catholic all my life. In my early years, I thought Jesus was a superhero, better than Superman. When I became a teenager, God became a rule maker and stern disciplinarian, just like Sr. Mercita ("Looks like a cheetah and growls like one too," we used to say about the nun at our school). God's voice was not merciful but full of judgment. My relationship with God had never matured beyond that between Almighty Creator and whiny, entitled teenager.

As I traveled through those seven endless days yelling at, begging, and bargaining with God, I realized that he was inviting me to grow up and form a new relationship with him. I kept running across the Bible verse from Jeremiah that stated, "For I know well the plans I have in mind for you—oracle of the LORD—plans for your welfare and not for woe, so as to give you a future of hope" (29:11). Friends had quoted that scripture to me all week long, it was on the parish bulletin my mom gave me when she brought Jonathan to visit us that week, and it was even engraved on a bracelet one of the PICU nurses was wearing. God was desperately trying to get my attention—I could not escape it. He wasn't punishing me or Jerry; he was allowing a situation that was somehow going to bring "a future of hope." He was asking me to trust him with my beautiful newborn daughter.

That's bananas. Crazy town. Insanity.

I'm not a big fan of suffering or pain and not particularly willing to accept misery and sorrow. And trusting in someone or something makes us vulnerable. In the past, every time I'd ever laid my vulnerability on the table, things had worsened. I felt like I was playing *Frogger*: fulfilling God's ask was like trying to cross a superhighway, dodging and weaving through the speeding cars. It was too much, and I couldn't do it.

Then I remembered the desperate deal I'd offered: *I'll take her any way you wish to give her to me, just don't let her die.* See where this is going? God had allowed Courtney to live. Awesome. He'd also allowed her to seize uncontrollably for no apparent reason. (Insert bad word here.) That's when I figured it out: if God was going to hold up his end of the "deal," then I had to keep mine. That meant that I'd have to trust him with my daughter's life and, as a bonus with purchase, my own.

It was seven days and nights before I managed to accept the deal I thought I was making. (I've since learned that things don't work this way when you're dealing with an almighty divinity who loves you eternally. God keeps his word, even when we don't.) God wasn't interested in extracting anything from me; he wanted me to trust him and to embrace his plan for our family, especially regarding my daughter. Once we dip a toe into this pond of trust and enter into a deeper relationship, God will ask a lot from us. He does this because he knows what we are capable of even when we don't. He wants us to trust him completely, not because it's good for him but because it's best for us. Trust gives us the grace we need to walk in faith that all shall be well. And when we don't trust, the lessons get harder and longer. Just ask me how I know.

I went all in with no idea where it would lead. In hindsight, this was a good thing. I had no idea what God would ask of me, but it hurt less to trust and surrender than to reach for control and be fearful. Some say (mothers and nuns, mostly) that a person will change only when the pain of staying in the same situation is greater than the perceived pain of change. I can attest to this truth. In that moment, I told God "enough" and laid down my heart, trusting, briefly, that he wouldn't crush it. At times,

I still struggle with trust; I am not who I was, but God is not finished with me yet.

HEART WORK

What about you? We all suffer. We all have struggles in our life, events that strip away our sense of control. But since control is an illusion, seeking it is essentially a giant neon sign saying you don't trust God to do what's best for you. I'm not talking about a menu plan for the week or your daily carpool schedule, although God can speak into those things as well.

When the big ask comes and you find yourself on your knees, completely unsure of what will happen with your next breath, your heart shattering into a million pieces and seized by indecision over the right thing to do, you have St. Paul's assurance that God will work all things together for the good of those who love him (see Romans 8:28). That doesn't mean that every last thing will be good. It means that as God works all things together, he will bring about what is good for you. And it won't necessarily be "good" the way you see it, but it will be the way God sees it.

How do we trust God? Hard work, my friend, and a little bit of heart work as well.

Have you ever had an experience where you felt helpless, alone, and scared that nothing would ever be the same? Take out your journal, the notes app on your phone, a napkin (preferably not one from a bar), or use the next page in this book. Start writing. Get it out of your head and in front of your heart. Ask yourself:

- *How is God allowing me to break today?*
- *What is he asking of me?*
- *What do I need to lay down at the foot of the Cross and allow his mercy and grace to seep into?*

Write it out. Draw it out. Give it to him. When we give our very selves, our children, our marriages, and our work over to God, miracles happen, peace abides, and we can be brave in the scared. We can survive the very worst that life brings us, and we can even do it with joy, because "for God all things are possible" (Mt 19:26).

MATTHEW 7:7-11

Ask, and it will be given to you; seek and you will find; knock and the door will be opened to you. For everyone who asks, receives; and the one who seeks, finds; and to the one who knocks, the door will be opened. Which one of you would hand his son a stone when he asks for a loaf of bread, or a snake when he asks for a fish? If you then, who are wicked, know how to give good gifts to your children, how much more will your heavenly Father give good things to those who ask him.

CHAPTER TWO

BLAME GAME

Choices. We have to make them every day. We choose what to make for dinner and whether to run an errand before picking up the kids. We also choose whether to look for a new job or move out of the city. Most of us sincerely try to do our best in any given situation.

The funny thing about choices is that one usually leads to the next, in both importance and complexity. Life insurance leads to wills and end-of-life planning. Paying bills leads to good credit and all the responsibilities that buying a car or owning a home entail. Having kids leads to choosing preschools and eventually colleges. Most of us believe that life is a school of decision-making: as we make each successive decision, we learn from the consequences and gain the knowledge to make a more informed and better decision the next time.

The problem with this belief is that it leaves us vulnerable and unprepared for an unforeseen outcome. It doesn't account for the fact that sometimes things go smoothly and sometimes they end badly for all involved—even when the direction we've chosen is a solid one. The challenge with all beliefs is that we often attach expectations to them. When we do, we limit our view of the whole picture. Our beliefs become our truth, and if those beliefs turn out to be false or even just partial, our truth collapses.

CONSEQUENCES

For many of us, that collapse means the unwelcome discovery that none of our previous, mature choices prepare us for the most important decisions we will be required to make. We go into the big challenges assuming that our options will be clear-cut and informed by the advice of experienced professionals. We don't allow for the possibility that even the best choices we make—with the very best intentions and with help from the very best professionals—can have dire consequences.

No one ever warns us that sometimes consequences can not only smell like spoiled milk, they can be catastrophic. If (and when) that happens, we're stripped of our confidence in our ability to make decisions. We lose faith in ourselves and in others. The truth we've been standing on is pulled out from under us, and we're left alone, binge-watching *Stranger Things*, surrounded by empty cans of orange soda, and speed-dialing Papa Giovanni's. Mine was usually large with extra cheese and pepperoni.

RESPONSIBLE ADULTS

Up until the onset of Courtney's seizures, the hardest decisions my husband and I had made involved which used car to buy, what movie we should see on a Friday night, and whether we needed life insurance. We thought we were "adulting" well. We had a family, we paid our bills on time, and we picked whole-life over term insurance (we've since learned our lesson there). We also attended Mass every Sunday. We were crushing the grown-up Catholic world.

None of that, however, prepared us for the exhaustion and fear that accompanied the sad realization that our daughter wasn't getting better and there was no definitive diagnosis. I had begged God to let me keep Courtney however he'd give her to me, yet I had no idea what "however" meant or would mean in the future.

Even more, I assumed that regardless of what "however" looked like, I'd be able to handle it and, in time, even fix it. We would overcome, and our story would show up in *Chicken Soup for the Soul*. Then we'd hit the talk show circuit and become a TV movie of the week. I'd already started my diet and picked out my award show dresses.

As you can guess by now, there were no talk shows or green room cupcakes or sparkly designer gowns. There wasn't even any weight lost. All we got were harder and harder choices.

DUE DILIGENCE

Life with Courtney continued to be unpredictable. Her seizures seemed to come every hour on the hour. We tried every available treatment to get them under control, but nothing worked. Despite the seizures, though, Courtney was a happy baby. Her smile could light up a room and her giggles gave me life. She loved it when Jonathan sang the "Winnie the Pooh" theme song. It made my heart sing to see them interact as if nothing was wrong.

Courtney's development was somewhat delayed due to the pharmaceutical cocktail she was taking. Still, she was slowly hitting the developmental markers of rolling over and getting on her hands and knees. An in-home physical and occupational therapist from our local early intervention program worked with her once a week. Doing everything I could to ensure a positive outcome for Courtney made it even harder for me to give up my desire for control.

One day in mid-June 1993, Courtney's neurologist found an anomaly during a regularly scheduled EEG. Suddenly, we had a possible diagnosis, and with that a treatment plan—a steroid with a high rate of success. It was not without controversy, though, due to the possible side effects. So we jumped into research mode.

We spoke to families whose children had done well with the treatment as well as families whose children had not. We turned over every rock we could doing due diligence for our daughter. We stepped outside the military system of medicine and got input from numerous leading specialists at major children's hospitals around the nation. We prayed and asked others to pray with us. After all, God had heard me once before; surely he would hear me again.

Although we never received a clear yes from God, we understood the lack of a no as a go-ahead. I was on a mission to save my daughter, after all, and I felt I'd been given the directive. This medication was going to change the course of Courtney's life and ours. I was filled with hope that maybe this time, with this treatment, we would get our daughter back. The seizures would stop, and our lives would be normal again. (I know—investing all our hope in this one medicine should've made us stop and think.)

We began administering the meds.

DISASTER

On day three—the Day Everything Changed—Courtney swelled up and couldn't breathe. We rushed her back to the ER. Her blood pressure tanked, then her kidneys decided to quit, and her brain swelled.

While the team took over, I stood in the corner hoping to disappear into the concrete. *What was going on? Why was this happening?* I had been so sure about this decision. Jerry and I had even prayed over this choice. Yes, I'd tried to fix my daughter. Yes, I'd wrestled back some control. Yes, even though God had let her live, I still wanted more for Courtney. But I was her mother. Wasn't it my job to try everything within my power to help her? Surely if this wasn't in the plan, God should have found a way to tell us, or warn us, or stop us, or . . . ?

MY FAULT

As I pressed myself against the cold, gray concrete, the team explained what was happening: Courtney was experiencing a rare allergic reaction to the steroid. She was one of the 2 percent of kids who could not withstand the treatment. This news impaled my heart. We'd been cautious. We'd done the research. Nothing unusual had shown up in the preliminary testing of the steroid. Still, all I could think was *I did this to her.*

A nurse rushed over to help me to a chair and ordered me to breathe. I almost blacked out. God had saved my child once, but now I had ruined everything. I had chosen to give her a drug that was killing her. In that moment, I just wanted to die.

Over the weeks that followed, Courtney remained puffy and swollen like the Michelin Man. She'd lost all of her previous physical and cognitive development and lay in her crib like a helpless newborn, whimpering and crying. The seizures kept coming, too. Nothing had improved; on the contrary, our daughter's condition had worsened. Courtney's allergic reaction had caused her brain to swell, permanently damaging her cortical nerves. Not only had I almost killed my daughter, but she'd never see my face again. She was diagnosed with what was then called permanent cortical blindness.

Up until the Day Everything Changed, Courtney had had a shot at a normal life. But when we left the hospital this time, we took with us a long list of things she would never do. The little hope we had was gone. In its place was a load of regret.

Forget about zombies. Nothing eats away at a person like guilt and blame.

I was also angry. There had been no warning alarms—good grief, even tornadoes come with those—and all we'd been told was that the treatment might not work. To make things worse, I couldn't escape the conclusion that God had abandoned us. If he was there at all, it felt like he was shaking his head and saying, "Courtney's life, as it was, wasn't good enough for you. You *had* to try and fix it. *You* made this bed, and now you'll have to lie in it."

My reply? "Burn the bed. I'll sleep on the floor."

ANGRY WITH GOD

That day, God and I entered what I call our wounded relationship phase. I was angry, so willing to throw gas on the fire of my rage, that I stopped all communication with God. Instead, I kept company with regret and guilt—harsh companions indeed—and punished myself for my false belief that Courtney's situation could have been improved. After all, God hadn't promised me *perfect*; he'd just promised me *not dead*. And that was where I had failed to be honest with myself. *Not dead* wasn't good enough for me.

As a result, I concluded, God had not only taken away my daughter's future but he'd also found a way to make me responsible for it. At least that is how I saw it at the time. And that is why I came closer to walking away from God that day than at any other moment in my life. I couldn't trust someone who hurt those I loved.

GOD REMAINED

Still, there was blessing in this mess. The world hates a vacuum: something has to fill the void besides dust bunnies the size of grapefruits—and that something can be faith in God. What kept my faith tethered to his mercy even though we weren't talking? What kept me believing when all I wanted was to unfriend him? Cowardice. My fear of being alone was even more powerful than my anger at God. Not my proudest moment, but the truth.

My grandmother always said that hindsight is twenty-twenty. It's taken me years to realize that while I was slamming my bedroom door in God's face, blocking him on all my spiritual social media sites, and sulking like a teenager, God never left me. And God never left Courtney.

On the Day Everything Changed, God made use of my fear to keep me close. He knew I didn't want to talk. He knew I wasn't ready to listen. But he also knew I wasn't going to walk away. In spite of my whining, stomping, and door slamming, he did what any good parent would do: God the Father remained, waiting patiently for me to grow up. In the meantime, God proved his presence in every disastrous choice by speaking words of encouragement through people I loved and trusted. I might not have been able to speak directly to him without screaming. My mom and dad, however, would gently suggest that I continue to go to Mass or say a Rosary. Each time I did as they asked (more out of obedience than from a desire to actually do it), peace came. God was there, loving me through the prayers of my childhood. Like my earthly parents, he stayed with me. He would not leave because that's what a loving parent does.

JESUS, I TRUST IN YOU

In the midst of crisis, it's hard to remember God's constancy. The adrenaline hits, and our brains go into fight-or-flight mode. The desperation we feel is as real as if we were racing away from a speeding car. We run, not walk, to safety. It takes time to process the horror of difficult moments, and God is often the last thing we think about.

Is it possible to change our immediate response, to push panic aside and let God in? Yes, but it takes time and practice. As with any habit, we must start with the small things so we can be ready for the big ones. If we can learn to calm ourselves in the simpler moments of stress—such as when the car gets a flat tire or the toilet overflows—we can begin to train ourselves to have a better response when things become truly serious.

Over the years, in moments of crisis, I've learned to pray "Jesus, I trust in you" over and over again. This simple prayer can calm our nerves, keep us present in the moment, and bring us the peace that allows room for solid decision-making. By repeating the word *trust*, we acknowledge that the Father will walk with us through whatever valley we tread.

Mental prayer makes space for God to do his thing in all situations. Choose a prayer from your childhood, a quote from a favorite saint, the Sign of the Cross, or the Glory Be. Practice saying it during small moments of difficulty so that you are able to place yourself in God's care immediately when a tidal wave hits. Automatic mental prayer will ease whatever hardship or challenge you're facing.

COULDA, WOULDA, SHOULDA

Now, be honest with yourself. Are you playing a blame game? Are there choices you feel guilty about? What regrets are you hiding in your heart right now? Can you find your way to letting them go? Not every decision you make will end the way you think it should, but strangely enough, that's okay.

Remember that taking responsibility isn't the same as taking blame. It took me a long time to figure out that when you play the blame game, nobody wins. We all regret decisions and second-guess our choices. That's part of our human frailty, and God understands this. But if we spend our lives playing coulda, woulda, shoulda, we'll miss out on God's bigger plan. His plan uses *every* choice for our good—even if we don't see it or understand it right away.

Remember, my friend, we see only what he allows us to see. There is so much more happening between the hidden layers of our lives. Maybe you've turned your back on God, as I did. But you can always choose to turn back toward the Father and, with the help of mental prayer, allow his face to shine upon you. If you can learn to trust him to guide your steps when little things go wrong, you'll begin to see that God the Father never abandons his children. Never.

PROVERBS 3:5-6

Trust in the Lord with all your heart,
   on your own intelligence do not rely;
In all your ways be mindful of him,
   and he will make straight your paths.

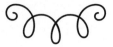

CHAPTER THREE

WHEN IT RAINS

Life can be a lot like dominoes. You get yourself all set up, and then, somehow, it all falls down. When something goes wrong, it never seems to be just one thing at a time. The car breaks down, and then the dishwasher leaks all over the kitchen floor. You fix one thing, only to have three other things fall apart. And you wonder who set the clock that it all happened at once.

The truth is that it didn't all happen at once. It only seems that way. Most things don't just happen overnight. In all likelihood, the things that catch you by surprise have been building over time. Perhaps you were unaware or inattentive. Perhaps you were preoccupied or too focused on whatever was on your radar to remember that there are usually a few things brewing *under* the radar.

Almost everyone has experienced a when-it-rains-it-pours season of life. But there are those chosen few who seem to live in a flood zone with constant downpours. If that's where you are, it's easy to forget that the sky is supposed to be blue. It's even easier to become pretty cynical about umbrellas.

OVERWHELMED

As Courtney turned two, I was tired of battling my fear of the future and embarked on a quest of self-sufficiency. I knew what needed to be done, and I did not trust anyone but myself to do it. I was an independent woman, dammit, one desperate to prove to myself that I was capable of being who my children needed no matter the personal cost. (Cue God's laugh track. Apparently, even the angels were in on the joke our lives had become!)

Courtney was beginning her second year on the ketogenic diet. Her grand-mal seizures came multiple times a day and at times she would stop breathing and begin to turn blue. For this reason, she could never be left alone, which was proving to be quite taxing on all of us. This medicinal diet had been effective in reducing the number of seizures, but it was a ton of work for me. It meant regimented mealtimes that included precisely measuring everything she'd eat and drink for the entire day. On top of the diet, Courtney had weekly therapy and doctor appointments and attended a special school for the severely disabled. She was still struggling to make any kind of developmental progress, remaining in the five- to seven-month-old range. Jerry was still on active duty in the navy *and* had begun a nighttime master's degree program. Add in our very active almost-five-year-old son, and my life defined the word *overwhelmed*.

From an early age, Jonathan was our smart, capable child. He taught himself to read at four and could tie his own shoes. He could entertain himself for hours, and I didn't have to worry about him. He attended preschool three days a week and brought home the requisite macaroni artwork. He was all about snack time, just like his dad. And he was very physically active. Jonathan also adored his sister. He'd play alongside her with his trains and superhero action figures. He would read her books, and when Courtney had a seizure, he'd hold her hand and tell her everything would be okay.

Have you ever taken a disabled child in a wheelchair to the park along with a fearless preschooler? Sure! Jumping off the top of the slide while pretending to be Batman? Why not! Swinging so high on the swings that the entire apparatus shook with the effort? Of course! On any given day, I looked like a BMX competitor, racing and running, popping wheelies with Courtney's wheelchair as I chased my daredevil son. To this day I have PTPS: post-traumatic playground syndrome. I still break out in a cold sweat whenever I see a swing set!

What I didn't see at the time was that Jonathan needed to socialize with his peers. He was so used to playing alone that when others came into the picture, he reacted like a long-tailed cat in a room full of rocking chairs. Jonathan also didn't handle transitions well; every day before school, he would throw tantrums and talk back. And because he'd learned to read at such a young age, he was quite articulate and had mastered the not-so-welcome art of sarcasm. I thought all this was normal, that he was just a chip off the ol' parental block.

THE ROAD OF DENIAL

So I let his troublesome behaviors go. I had too many other things to worry about; I didn't want to have to worry about Jonathan too. I was determined to keep my you-know-what together and conquer life, and I didn't want anyone to think that just because I had a special needs child, I couldn't handle my son.

The problem with letting things go and not trusting anyone to help is that ignoring problems only makes them grow. And they don't grow into fragrant flowers. They become messy weeds with deep roots and thorny stems that become nearly impossible to pull out on your own.

The Halloween he was four, I went into Jonathan's preschool with a tray of pumpkin cupcakes. Courtney was safely at her school, and I was happy to be "snack mom" for Jonathan's class. I didn't often get the chance to help out at his school, and I wanted to make a good impression.

Upon my arrival, Jonathan proudly showed me his cubby, where his Thomas the Tank Engine backpack hung. He introduced me to three little friends and beamed with joy. I was surprised when his teacher asked me to step out into the hallway with her while the aides set up for the party.

"Mrs. Lenaburg, I'm concerned about Jonathan. He's not getting along with the other students, and he refuses to share. He also has a temper." Her face looked like a pinched prune, and I became instantly defensive. Despite my racing heart, I spouted every excuse for my son's behavior and smiled my face off. I hid my fisted hands behind my back.

Horse manure, I thought. *Jonathan is fine.*

I thanked her for telling me and told her I'd discuss the situation with my husband. No one was going to convince me there was anything to worry about with Jonathan. I put the conversation out of my mind and handed out cupcakes. And so began the long road of denial. That evening I discussed the situation with Jerry. He simply advised me to do what I thought best, so I did. I left it alone.

As the weeks passed, I began to notice little things at home and when we were out: an hour-long meltdown over not having chocolate milk at lunch; ripping a page out of his coloring book when he thought his coloring wasn't neat enough; refusing to share anything with anyone, especially at the library or the neighborhood playground. Still, Jerry and I figured Jonathan was just strong-willed—like his parents.

In December, the preschool administrator called. She asked to see both Jerry and me *immediately.* I panicked. *Was Jonathan okay? Why did we need to come now?* An hour later, Jerry and I were sitting in two small chairs with our knees up to our chins while she informed us that our son had bitten another student and that Jonathan would no longer be welcome at the school.

Simple and to the point—like a dagger to my heart. I was mortified and speechless. My head felt hot and my hands shook. Jerry was stone silent sitting there in his dress blues. No one moved. It was awkward and horrible.

Finally, the administrator rose from her little chair and opened the door. Jonathan, wearing his oversized Thomas the Tank Engine backpack, stood there with tears in his eyes. I saw no sympathy in the administrator's face. I got up, knocking over that little chair, and said nothing as I left, dragging my crying child behind me. Jerry followed in silence.

ALONE AND IN TROUBLE

As I write this now, many years later, one thing that stands out is that nowhere during this time of overwhelming denial and pain did I ask for God's help. I refused to see myself as weak and in need, even when—especially when—I was.

Jerry drove back to work, and I put Jonathan in the van and headed to Courtney's school. Then I started yelling. I lost my temper and berated my four-year-old son, saying things I could never take back. I pulled it together long enough to get Courtney out of school and into the van. As I closed the van door, Jonathan reached for me from his booster seat and said with tears in his eyes, "I'm sorry, Mama." I'd like to say that I stopped the insanity and took him into my arms and had a good cry with him in that school parking lot. But that would be a lie. Instead I said, "You should be," and closed the van door. We drove home in silence.

When we got home, I settled the kids in front of cartoons and went to the kitchen. After some serious ice cream therapy, I unpacked Jonathan's backpack and opened his parent/teacher notebook. In it, I saw the truth. Jonathan had been struggling with his temper, and the teacher was frustrated with our inaction. I can honestly say that I don't remember reading half those notes before that day. I'd signed the book's entries but evidently hadn't paid much attention to them.

Panic set in hard and fast, as did self-centeredness. My criticism turned inward. Obviously, I was a horrible mother. It was bad enough that Courtney was different. Now Jonathan had issues. Maybe I should let my mother raise the kids. I was *not* going to be the mother of two atypical kids.

I had ignored the signs of Jonathan's distress because we were in constant crisis management mode with Courtney. This life was too much for one person to handle. (See how I said "person," not "couple"? Yeah. That's a few chapters away.) So I did what any crazed daughter would do. I called my mom and poured out my heart, expecting support and validation. Instead, she confirmed everything the teacher and administrator had said. And the moment she mentioned God? I hung up. I felt betrayed and even more isolated than before.

REVELATIONS

That night during bath time, Jonathan was unusually quiet. As I tucked him into bed, I asked if he wanted to say his bedtime prayers. When we came to the part where we asked God to help other people, he whispered, "Please, God, don't let Mommy give me away. I'm very sorry for biting S., and I promise never to do it again. Please, God, make Mommy love me like she loves Courtney."

Damn. Damn. Damn.

My heart caught in my throat, and tears threatened to fall. Jonathan's folded hands were clenched and shaking. His big hazel eyes looked up at me, terrified. *My son was afraid of me? He didn't trust me to take care of him? He didn't think that I loved him as much as I loved his sister?* I couldn't take the fear in his eyes anymore. I gently asked his permission to hold him in my arms. He nodded yes.

I sat Jonathan in my lap and rocked back and forth. I told him that I was very sorry I had yelled and that I had had a very bad day, just like Alexander in one of his favorite children's books. Over and over again, I told him how much I loved him, that I loved him even more than Courtney because God gave him to me first. Through the tears, I did my best to reassure him that I wasn't going to give him away. Not ever. He whispered, "Don't worry, Mommy. Jesus will help you."

NOT ALONE

Sometimes, when you think you already have all you can handle, God allows even more. That night he used my son's words to remind me that I didn't have to do this alone. He'd been there the whole time, waiting for me to invite him in. He knew the only way I'd listen to his voice again was through the painful honesty of my son's earnest prayer.

I'm a stubborn, bull-headed woman, and that personality trait has served me well for the majority of my life. Sometimes, however, it makes entering into a conversation with the Lord challenging. It makes trusting him and his plan for my life nearly impossible, especially when I want things the way I want them and am not open to any other possibilities.

I struggled to ask God into my life because my pride wouldn't allow me to acknowledge I was drowning. I didn't listen to God's answers because I didn't trust that he had any answers I *wanted* to hear. It's as though I was on a sinking boat and tossed the life jacket away. To me, asking for help meant dependence, and dependence meant weakness. I was afraid of being weak.

I'd had it all wrong. Through my four-year-old, I learned that we are not meant to walk through this life alone. The Bible tells us that we "have the strength for everything through him who empowers us" (Phil 4:13). But after we ask him in, the hard part begins. Once we open the door, once we allow him to heal our hurts from the inside out, we still need to learn how to depend on him. And how does that dependence begin? Through trust.

God hadn't fixed Courtney and had allowed me to break Jonathan. Honestly, I didn't trust God to make my grocery list, much less heal my life. But he didn't give up on me. Instead, he showed me the pain I had caused my sweet son. Then he showed me, through Jonathan, that I needed help and needed it right then. If I didn't relinquish my stubborn, prideful behavior, things would only get worse.

Tears still well in my eyes when I think of that night.

ON YOUR OWN?

Because I didn't trust God, I placed my need to feel independent ahead of him. I desired self-sufficiency more than anything else, even to the detriment of my own child. That's just crazy town, friends. It's insane to think that it's even possible to take care of everyone's needs without God walking alongside you, encouraging you and lifting you up every step of the way.

Does the pain in your life make you feel like a failure? Are you at peace with your own limitations, or do you feel as if you need to look strong, maybe even perfect? It took me a long time to appreciate how God made me. He created a woman with enough spunk and fire to advocate for her special needs daughter, to handle long deployments separated from her husband, and to love her son just as he was. I just had to believe that I could trust God to help me.

When we believe that we have to handle everything on our own strength and that we are willing to do anything to handle everything, we are standing on the edge of the abyss with our big toe hanging over. It's a toxic mixture of fear and pride—pride that you can do everything on your own power and fear that you will step off that cliff and never stop falling.

I did not want to acknowledge that once I asked God into the mess, the difficult process of transformation would begin. I would need to trust him with the rebuilding and the restoration of my life. I was once again being asked to let go of control. I had done it more than once, but each time it seemed that the chunks of life I was being asked to surrender were bigger and bigger.

What about you, my friend? How are you handling the hard in your life? Is there something you keep trying to handle on your own? Have you refused help or been too ashamed to ask for it?

Don't believe the lie the Deceiver whispers into your ear—the lie that you don't need God, that you are better off without him. The rain does come. Sometimes, it feels as though it will never end. Tell God you need him. (He already knows that anyway.) Put out your hand, my friend, and allow Christ to lift you up from the mud. I promise you will not regret the choice to take his hand in trust.

SIRACH 2:1, 5-6

My child, when you come to serve the Lord,
    prepare yourself for trials. . . .
For in fire gold is tested,
    and the chosen, in the crucible of humiliation.
Trust in God, and he will help you;
    make your ways straight and hope in him.

CHAPTER FOUR

RUNNING ON EMPTY

Where do you turn when you've got nothing left? To prayer? To the saints? To God? *Every* time? If one of those options is your answer, you're definitely holier than I am. If it isn't, keep reading.

Why is it that when we're sinking deep in the mire we instinctively reach for things we *know* won't help us? Heck, we even reach for the things we *know* will *hurt* us! It's easy to justify. All we have to do is tell ourselves that we deserve it; that we need a break; that we're doing something for us; or that it just doesn't matter (even though it does).

In the midst of all of the stress and strife we encounter, it's understandable if we feel less than wonderful about the dawn of another day. Nevertheless, many of us tend to deny the emotional and spiritual price we've been paying. We get up dreading what the day might bring but bury the dread under smiley-faced inspirational quotes. Inside, we're empty, and we know it. We just hope and pray that nobody else does.

DEEP-FRIED HELL

After I reconciled with Jonathan, there was more peace in our home, or at least the illusion of peace. I felt steadier than I had in several weeks. We had to make a decision before the new year, but I had no idea what we were going to do about Jonathan and his schooling. Our options were limited to public school or private school kindergarten, but I was not convinced that Jonathan could emotionally handle either of those environments. So we let our budget do the talking and sent him to public school.

Jerry was pulling further away emotionally. He was a good provider and would assist with chores around the house. He even handled bath time with the kids every night, which was a gift to me. But we weren't talking about anything beyond what was for dinner or the kids' schedules. We were just going through the motions of life. Our marriage registered low on the emotional connection meter. It just seemed like too much effort to dig through all the hurt and pain we were going through, so we didn't.

Courtney's seizures continued; her medical picture was becoming more complicated by the day. Our extended families were screaming opinions, and the noise of our life was becoming too much to handle. Did I turn to God in my hour of need? Nope, I turned to the Golden Arches and the gospel according to Wendy's. The Big Mac would be my savior, I just knew it. I was quick to forget that God was available for the assist, so I turned to the one place I knew would not judge me.

You might say that stress and I did not get along well, and you would be right. When the pressure became too intense, I ate. There is something very comforting about food, especially a burger and fries piping hot from the deep-fat fryer with a sprinkle of salt. Add in a chocolate shake, and this girl is in heaven. It took me a while to figure out that being lost in a sea of deep-fried food and self-loathing actually isn't much like heaven at all.

Sadly, this stress eating was nothing new. The first time I engaged in binge eating was in high school, when I failed my freshman algebra class. I knew that my parents were going to lose their minds over it, so I hit the local convenience store on my way home from school and bought a half gallon of mint chocolate chip ice cream and a family-size bag of nacho cheese chips. By the time I reached home, half the bag of chips was gone, and the ice cream was calling my name. Before dinner I had eaten half the ice cream. Alas, I still had to face my parents' disappointment. Then, instead of accepting responsibility for my poor study habits and asking for help, I turned my self-loathing into another binge eating session later that night.

FOOD AND LOVE

In my home growing up, food equaled love. Dinnertime meant tasty meals that my mother put together on a very tight budget. She was never a fan of cooking but knew that with a family of ten there would be no getting around it. So she dove in and provided my siblings and me with some wonderful memories shared at the big round table in our very tired kitchen.

Food also loomed large in my dating life with Jerry. I sent boxes of cookies and brownies to him when he was at the Naval Academy and in flight school. Pretty much every date involved sharing a meal. I discovered early in my relationship with Jerry that the way to his heart was definitely through his stomach. So I spent hours in the kitchen making sure that my guy knew how loved he was. Again, food equaled love.

That is why I turned to food when life was great and when life was horrible. Whether we were celebrating or mourning, food was part of it. No matter the occasion, I made sure that there was cake or at least ice cream.

In the weeks after Jonathan's removal from preschool, my drive-through habit grew out of control. The evidence was all over my car. There were wrappers everywhere, not only fast food but also my favorite Hostess snacks. All eaten in secret. I figured the drive-through was cheaper than therapy. Besides, if you went to therapy, people would think you were broken, and there was no way *anyone* was going to judge me as being broken. For the record, a Big Mac doesn't judge.

THE WEIGHT OF IT ALL

I was ashamed and didn't want to let people into my shame. I had always been a people-pleasing perfectionist, but suddenly I couldn't please anyone—my husband, my son's teachers, my parents. Everything was falling apart around me, and I couldn't stop it or fix it. I used food to numb my pain and control my panic. I would eat until I felt sick to my stomach and then eat some more.

I gained thirty pounds in two months, and I did not care. Courtney was two and a half, and I was still wearing my maternity jeans. I was at a fork in the road (Get it? *Fork* in the road . . .), and in complete denial about how I was dealing with things. As the convergence of Courtney's needs, Jonathan's trauma, and my husband's emotional distance took their toll on my own emotional and mental health, I didn't ask for help. I turned to food for the comfort and love I craved.

It seemed to me that I had few alternatives. I had tried to reach out to Jerry, but he was holed up in the basement night after night working on his master's thesis. I was needy, too needy to recognize that Jerry was having his own struggles. I was also too fragile to risk rejection. And you know what? The Golden Arches never rejected me. They always greeted me with a smile and hot food that made me feel fulfilled—for about ten minutes. After that, not so much.

FOOD AND FAILURE

One night, after an argument with Jerry over what to do about Jonathan, I sat and watched movies while bingeing on nacho cheese chips and ice cream (salt and sweet, the therapy combo of champions). I had felt horrible before, but that night I hit a wall. My mind flashed back to my high school experience, and I sat on the couch staring at the empty ice cream container. All I wanted to do was throw up.

I quietly went to the bathroom and tried for more than thirty minutes to make myself puke. I hated to vomit, but I was desperate, so I just kept trying. It couldn't be *that* hard. I went so far as to drink the *entire* bottle of ipecac I had in case Jonathan got into something he shouldn't. Nothing. I failed. I couldn't even *vomit* like a normal person. I was failing over and over again, every single day. I sat on the cold hard bathroom floor and wept. Jerry found me curled up there on the floor two hours later.

I tried to explain how empty I felt inside and how afraid I was that I was going to ruin our kids and that he would leave me and . . . and . . . and. He looked at me with a mix of confusion and pity in his eyes and simply said, "Maybe you should go on a diet. It might help you feel better. You have kind of let yourself go."

In that moment, I felt such hatred toward him. I stood up and went to bed in silence. I don't think we exchanged words for three days. I didn't need a diet. I needed love and acceptance. Apparently, I wasn't going to find that in Jerry. Of course, I thought this was the lowest of the low. Nope, it actually got worse.

HIGH SCHOOL REUNION

The next night was my ten-year high school reunion. You know, the one you go to with a huge chip on your shoulder hoping to prove to all the naysayers that you actually *are* somebody and that your life has turned out to be even better than a fairy tale.

I was the heaviest I had been since giving birth to Jonathan five years earlier. My mom went shopping with me and bought me a suit at Dress Barn. The irony of buying clothes at a store with the word *barn* in its name never occurred to me. Aside from emergency liposuction and plastic surgery, there was no changing my size, so I was all in. Besides, the suit looked good even if I didn't.

It was prom night for twenty-seven-year-olds, and I actually felt pretty. I had gotten my hair cut, and Jerry had treated me to getting my nails done. The plan was for my BFF from high school and her husband to meet us there. There would be dancing and cocktails, and I was excited to see a few people. I was also nervous and unsure how others had changed in ten years. But that was fine—I would get to show off my naval aviator to the world; no one needed to know that our marriage was not perfect. It was game on: I wore three girdles to keep my drive-through habit in place and a big smile pasted on my face, all camouflaging the truth. I felt prepared for anything, ready to conquer the world and the class of 1985.

It was a disaster. Every time someone asked about my kids, I fumbled over how to convey that I had a special needs daughter. I felt just as out of place as I had my first day as a freshman. I slipped into the ladies' room to escape my own awkwardness. While attending to business, I overheard a conversation that confirmed my worst fears and blew my blissful illusions right out of the water.

"Did you see that suit? Who wears a suit to a reunion? Did she not get the memo? It's a cocktail party. Geez. And she looks like a puffed-up blowfish. Yikes. Did you hear that there's something wrong with her kid?" It went on and on, their voices dripping in pity and spite. When I finally got up the nerve to leave the stall, the two lovely ladies were still there fixing their perfect hair and chatting about their perfect lives. I simply opened the door, washed my hands, and left them staring at me open-mouthed.

ENOUGH AND NOT ENOUGH

Instead of feeling vindicated at their visible embarrassment, I felt crushed. Their words screamed the truth. I wasn't hiding anything. My shame and dysfunction were hanging out for all to see. I would never be enough. I was a joke, and I knew it. I found Jerry in the crowd, and we left. I was silent all the way home, even though he kept asking what was wrong. I changed, grabbed some ice cream, and began a movie marathon. Jerry grew tired of badgering me and went to bed.

I never slept that night. Instead, I ate a half gallon of ice cream and an entire box of Girl Scout cookies and threw that brand-new suit in the trash. The entire time, all I kept thinking was that those two women were exactly right about everything. I had a pitiful excuse for a life, and "Failure" was my middle name. I hadn't been enough in 1985, and I still wasn't enough in 1995. I proved that point to myself over and over with every spoonful of chocolate hate.

What is it to be "enough"? I wasn't smart like my brothers and sister. I wasn't pretty or accomplished in any way. My entire identity was wrapped up in being Jerry's wife and Jonathan and Courtney's mom, and none of that was going very well. I could not wrap my head around the fact that the ideal life I had created in my mind—and just *knew* was meant to be—was simply not going to happen. There would be no picket fence and no perfect children—and *it was all my fault*.

Instead of figuring out how to let go of self-hatred and the deep disappointment I had about my life, I took something I loved and used it to punish myself. Food was readily accessible to me, and I could hide my pain behind a well-baked loaf of pumpkin bread. No one had to know that I had already eaten one of the two loaves I had baked. I hid the evidence quite well, but my shame meter reading climbed with each bite. There would be no diet for me, just more self-medicating with chocolate, more stuffing down my feelings with whatever tasted good.

BURYING THE PAIN

In the midst of my misery, I chose to ignore the pull of my heart to seek a relationship with God. The stirring was there, but I just shoved it down to make room for the next pan of brownies. That was easier, I thought, than facing the pain of being rejected and judged yet again. Instead of trusting God, I ran straight to the drive-through to hide from the hard, from the pain, and from my perceived failures as a wife, a mother, and a woman. The food did nothing but bury the pain, which made it more difficult to dig up and heal it.

And God? He already knew it all. He was still chasing me and telling me, "Stop! I already love you just the way you are, in your mess, in your pain." But I just kept running, or in my case, rolling up to ask for a number one with large fries.

I knew that if I asked Jesus into the mess, something would have to change, and I was not ready for that. Change demands two things: surrender and a willingness to do the hard work required. Surrender was not going to happen, even though I knew it was my path to freedom. Instead, I let fear and self-loathing keep me right where I was. *How could God love this wreck of a human?* Every time I even considered letting go and letting God, hard things would come, and my fragile illusion of peace would disintegrate. As for hard work, I figured I had done more than my share of that. I was not going to volunteer for even more hard work. But think: if you want those awesome abs, you need to do a lot of intense work at the gym. I was not prepared to lift anything more than another chocolate shake.

Self-medication with food (or alcohol, drugs, etc.) does not bring authentic God-given peace—just more anger and self-destruction. I looked to food for the love I was searching for and felt emptier than ever. I was digging myself into a hole it would take decades to escape. It seemed as if there was no peace in my life unless I was baking, but that was only a lie I allowed myself to believe. I just kept running away from what I feared was the truth about my life, one chocolate chip cookie at a time (okay, ten).

Self-hatred and self-pity, fueled by guilt and anger, can lead to isolation and loneliness. Isolation is the worst feeling in the world. It distorts your view of everything, especially your own self-worth. The Deceiver whispers the lie that you are unworthy of love and wants you to stay in that state of confusion and delusion. He wants you as far away from the light of truth as possible.

MORE THAN ENOUGH

Whatever our disappointment, disillusionment, or pain, the love and acceptance we are searching for is found only at the foot of the Cross. God's sacrifice is greater than our greatest shame. There is no substitute for him. He is my beloved and yours, waiting for you and me with arms open. His mercy and healing are more than enough. The Song of Songs says, "You are beautiful in every way, my friend, there is no flaw in you!" (4:7). So why did I feel like my body and soul were covered with acne?

As I surrendered my daughter and my son to God a little at a time, he kept asking for more, and I kept telling him it was enough. Standing before God, I felt naked and afraid. All I wanted was to hide the shame that was already known to him. I had not yet learned that surrendering to God allows him to handle all the big feelings. God permitted me to experience the cost of choosing not to surrender to him. Once again, I had a decision to make. I could have chosen to be brave in the scared and allow his love to conquer my fear. I didn't.

LET GOD HAVE IT

What are you trying to hide from God? What is the source of your humiliation and regret? What are you using to avoid dealing with disappointment and pain? Shine a light on it and offer it back to him as a gift of gratitude in return for his sacrifice on the Cross. You don't need to be punished. He already paid the price so you don't have to.

What are you really looking for, and where are you looking for it? What do you fear will happen if you surrender all your struggles and disappointments to God? Aren't you tired of doing it all on your own? If it takes screaming and yelling at God to turn over your hurt, go ahead and howl—he's a big God and can take it.

I don't know about you, my dear friend, but I find that emotional exhaustion isn't pretty, and shame and regret are ugly too. God stands ready to forgive, renew, and redeem. Do it now: put down the milkshake (or drug or drink), and pick up the banner of truth. Know that you are enough, just as you are, and that God loves you right now.

MATTHEW 13:46

When he finds a pearl of great price, he goes and sells all that he has and buys it.

CHAPTER FIVE

THE LIES WE TELL OURSELVES

Most of us go through life thinking that we are basically honest. We don't rob banks, we don't cheat on our taxes, and we return lost things to their rightful owners. Generally, we tell the truth.

We also don't consider ourselves gullible. We think we can tell when someone is lying. We're pretty sure we know when something is too good to be true. And we can smell the baloney a mile away.

Except when it comes to the lies we tell ourselves. What are they? How about these for starters: *I am in control of my life/my family/my friends/my health/my job/my fill-in-the-blank; I don't deserve to be loved; God could never forgive me; I really need this drink/drug/donut; I am a lost cause; I can quit anytime I want to; this problem will go away on its own; nothing will ever get better.* Have you heard any of these echoing in your heart? These are the sorts of lies we find it very easy to believe. Because we mistake them for the truth, we tell them to ourselves more than we know. And we fall for them, almost every time.

When you allow God in and begin to risk trusting him, these lies cannot stand. One by one, they begin to crumble in the light of his truth. The Bible says that "the truth will set you free" (Jn 8:32). First, though, it can make you pretty miserable. That is especially true when you realize that you've been telling yourself a whole lot of lies just to keep from having to face it.

GROWING APART

In the fall of 1995, my dad, Joe, was in the middle of chemo round three and was struggling mightily. He had been exposed to Agent Orange during his tour in Vietnam and had been diagnosed with non-Hodgkin's lymphoma when I was pregnant with Courtney three years earlier. Dad was a fighter by nature and was not going to give up, but the treatment was taking a heavy toll on him.

Pain had found its way into every aspect of my life. I could not escape it. Not only was Courtney still suffering daily seizures, but now I had to watch my dad, who had always been as strong as an ox, deal with nausea and neuropathy. He and Courtney spent many a weekend hanging out on the couch together. She snuggled into his arms between seizures, and he tried to remain positive despite the great pain.

Jerry remained distant. It was as if he were standing outside the arena, just waiting for the contest of pain to end. Entering into the fray took too much out of him, so he walked the perimeter. I allowed it because every time I pushed, Jerry would close yet another emotional door. I gave up begging him for attention. Besides, everything else seemed more urgent than my relationship with my husband.

It felt as though the two of us were slowly coming apart at the seams. It was a gradual uncoupling, a gentle tug on the thread from the hem of a sweater that would eventually lead to a great unraveling. Our marriage seemed destined to be discarded, tossed aside in a pile of jumbled-up, knotted threads.

WHERE TO TURN?

Jerry was working all kinds of crazy hours as a naval officer, and because most evenings were taken up with his studies, I had little to no support with the kids. With everything going on with my dad and the kids, I was tapped out emotionally on a daily basis. I used food to comfort my very lonely heart. This led to mood swings and weight gain, which in turn led to more emotional overeating. It was a vicious cycle.

I would try to occupy myself at night with crafting projects and reading the latest romance novel, losing myself in the epic adventures. I'd put myself in the book mentally, replacing the heroine in the beautiful romance. I was desperate to escape from my lonely reality.

Marriage is hard. This most intimate of friendships is like a garden. It needs daily tending, with proper watering and weeding, in order to cultivate the possibility of beauty springing to life between two people whom God made for each other. If you allow the weeds to continue to grow without killing them, they will choke the life out of the fruitful plants, and slowly but surely, your garden will die.

LONGING FOR LOVE

My marriage was in need of some serious watering. Jerry and I had been living through one hell of a drought, and I yearned for the days of our courtship: the simple walks by the waterfront in Annapolis; the late-night runs to Chick and Ruth's Delly for chocolate milkshakes; just the two of us laughing and talking for hours on end. He had been so attentive when we were dating and in our first year or so of marriage. The passion and spark that had drawn Jerry and me to one another five years earlier was waning, and I had no idea what to do about it.

One spring evening, feeling lonely after I had put the kids to bed, I went downstairs to find Jerry, who had been writing a paper. As I came down the steps, I noticed that his computer screen had no words on it. He was turned away from me, so I took a few more steps into the room and realized that he was looking at photos of naked women. Several had more than one woman in the frame. I called his name, and he jumped in his chair, shutting the screen off before turning around. His actions said more than words ever could. The look on his face sealed the deal. He was ashamed. He did not want me to know what he was doing.

I had never really thought about porn before that night. I knew about racy magazines, and I had even seen a photo or two in high school. (It was embarrassing and made me feel like I could never measure up.) I had just set the images aside and moved on with life. Some of Jerry's guy friends would occasionally mention a model's name or the month she had appeared in "that magazine," and each time I brushed it off. I knew that they watched certain movies, and some of his buddies even frequented strip clubs. This was just part of the military culture, I thought. It was just boys being boys—until one of those boys lived in my house and slept in my bed.

Rule number one of marriage survival: if you are not prepared to go to battle right then and there, retreat immediately, and save the fight for another day. I pretended that I hadn't seen anything and that Jerry hadn't either. Jerry had no problem with that.

A LOOK IN THE MIRROR

Sadly, this scene repeated itself over and over for months. I began to pull away from my husband physically, feeling threatened by the images floating on the screen and now implanted in my own mind. The conclusion was logical and straightforward: Jerry didn't find me to be enough. Fear once again began to squeeze my heart.

I finally got brave one night and took a long, hard look at myself in the mirror. My pregnancies had changed my body permanently. The emotional overeating I used to manage the daily pressure of meeting Courtney and Jonathan's needs put an even greater strain on my body. And I was older.

The stretch marks, the swollen tummy, and all things swoopy and droopy lay bare in front of my eyes. Mirrors do not lie, but the way we see what's in the mirror often does. I was totally unprepared for the emotional upheaval my reflection unleashed in my mind.

Not only was what I saw *not* the body of the twenty-one-year-old my husband had married, but it looked to me like the body of a haggard old woman who had decided that chips and ice cream were better than an antidepressant. This body appeared weak and soft to me, unable to carry the current weight of my life. This body made me angry, and I wanted to kick the mirror into a thousand pieces. I didn't do it only because I couldn't afford seven more years of even worse luck. The hardest part was that I felt completely powerless to change what I saw in that mirror. Any of it.

THE BIGGEST LIE

The pressures on our marriage came to a head that summer as Courtney turned three. The August heat drove me downstairs one night to the cool of the basement. There sat Jerry, his nightly ritual of images flashing across the screen. He heard me and turned the screen off, as always, acting as if nothing were amiss. I pulled a chair up next to his desk, gave him some baloney about how we shared everything, and asked why he was hiding this.

I was failing at motherhood, but I would not fail at marriage. No way was I going to be left alone. I had become obsessed in the previous few weeks with not allowing Jerry and me to join the 80 percent of couples with a severely disabled child who end up divorcing. No matter what it took, I was determined to keep us in the 20 percent. I turned the screen back on with bold determination, telling Jerry that I was not intimidated by what I saw. It was the biggest lie I ever told in my lifetime, but there was no turning back now. We began to look at the images together each night, and fell into a deeper pit of despair under the guise of trying to make our marriage work.

DOOR TO DARKNESS

Instead of helping Jerry to find the grace he needed to step away from his sin, I opened the door to sin wider. I rationalized it by telling myself that if this was what he needed to stay in our marriage and not abandon me, then I was bound and determined to provide for his every need. In time, photos were not enough, and we moved into films. One evening, I allowed Satan to enter our marriage bed: while a film was playing in the background, we entered into the most intimate act between a husband and wife. Jerry never made eye contact with me.

The truth of what I had allowed shattered my heart. I had chosen sin over sanity; the evil I thought I could keep secret over the light of truth. Shame crashed down in a way that I have never, ever forgotten. Jerry was not making love to me—he was with her, and I was just the poor physical substitute. She was flawless, and I was nothing but flaws. She was perfection, and I was pitiful. That night showed me how empty our marriage had become. In my fear, I had agreed to it all.

When we're trapped in denial, the dominoes in our lives continue to fall. Problems cascade into even more problems, and we become less and less able to resist temptation and sin. It took only one night to open the door to seven years of darkness before God would show us the way out. Fear is a liar. It slithers its way into the nooks and crannies of your heart and clouds your judgment. It can convince you to choose a path that leads straight to hell's doorstep.

TRUTH AND BEAUTY

Fear and anxiety make it easy to believe the lies we tell ourselves and the rationalizations we make for doing what we know is wrong. Only the grace and redemption of God can repair the wreckage of such choices.

The marital embrace is a most powerful act. It can build a marriage or be its point of destruction. In those seven years, Jerry and I denied our God-given dignity, degraded the beauty of our marriage covenant, and defiled our marriage bed. We used our grief and sadness over life's difficulties and challenges to justify the sinful choices we made instead of surrendering those struggles to God. We did not allow him to show us the beauty and truth of our married love.

We were not leading each other to God at all. Instead, we encouraged each other into the trap of lust and lies. We set on fire the gift of intimacy presented to us the day we married. Turning our backs on God, we refused the restorative power of authentic self-giving love to soften the blows that the world was handing out like free candy. Still, God's mercy waits in the place where sinners fall.

In time, God showed me that denying reality leads us into secrecy and sin. But while I continued to forge ahead on my own path of self-destruction, God remained patient and present, waiting for me to trust him with all I was refusing to accept. God's love for me and my husband would have been enough to strengthen us to face the truth of our own weakness. If we had been able to admit how much we needed God and each other, we would have stopped using each other and found genuine freedom and love many years earlier.

NO SECRETS

Why do we try so hard to hide our pain and our shame from God, turning to sin instead of the safety of his arms? After all, he already knows everything we have done: every lie told, every deception and manipulation engineered, and every lustful thought and act. He is *God,* omnipotent and omniscient. He knows every thought we have had or will have, and every action we have taken or have yet to take. He knows us inside out and upside down. Why do we try to cover up what he already knows?

Is there a deep, dark secret you are keeping? Have you been afraid to accept the truth that could set you free? Are you willing to allow God into your pain? Are you able to consider, for just a moment, that what you've been telling yourself isn't true?

Perhaps you are stuck in the same darkness that Jerry and I were in. If that's the case, I encourage you to ask God into the shame, sin, and regret. Invite him to heal, restore, and redeem. Allow God's restorative light to shine into the darkest corner of your shame, and you will no longer be a slave to it. There is a way out. You are more than your greatest shame, my friend. All things are possible with God, so be free. Freedom is his gift. God gave it to me, and he gave it to our marriage. He will give it to you as well.

PROVERBS 28:13

Those who conceal their sins do not prosper,
but those who confess and forsake them obtain mercy.

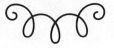

CHAPTER SIX

ACCEPTANCE

When it comes to difficult situations, *acceptance* is a word we bandy about a lot. But how many of us think deeply about what acceptance really means for us? When something doesn't go as expected, or when life takes a turn for the worse, most of us throw our hands up and ask, "Really, God? What are you thinking?" Or my favorite: "Why me, God?" Very few of us are quick to board the acceptance bus and willingly tolerate, let alone welcome, suffering or struggle.

Still, everyone experiences hardship because it's part of the human condition, brought about by original sin. No matter how good we are, or if we have followed every one of God's commandments (which no one can ever do, so please don't brag about it or stress out about it), we *all* fall short of God's glory and we *all* suffer. We don't choose our trials, but when a trial comes, we're offered a choice: we can fuss and complain about the injustice in this world, or we can . . . wait for it . . . accept it.

Does anyone go around saying "Bring it on!" to life's challenges? Of course not. At heart, we are all pretty self-centered people who want what we want, when and how we want it. And we want it without challenges. Most of us will do almost anything to avoid dealing with adversity. The irony is that we are also people of faith, and we know that bad things do happen to good people (the book of Job, anyone?). We just wish bad things would never happen to us.

Back to our choice. It is our pride—our desire to be in control and fix the situation—that directs us to fight *against* instead of *through* trials. Fighting through challenges allows us to accept the reality of a difficult situation *without having the ability to change it.* Oddly enough, fighting against challenges ourselves—alone—doesn't help us avoid the pain; it simply puts off and prolongs the misery. But acceptance doesn't come easy.

TUG-OF-WAR

By 1999, I'd been trying to fix my daughter for seven years, and this tug-of-war with God for control of the situation had taken its toll on every aspect of my life. I'd give whatever the current struggle was over to God for a time, and then, when things didn't go my way, I would rip it back out of his hands.

Every time I thought I had reached a place of peace, God allowed another trial, and I would grapple once again, like a Greco-Roman wrestler trying to strong-arm the Lord of the universe for control over the outcome. Needless to say, I did not come out on the winning side . . . ever.

Around this time, Jerry left active duty in the navy, and we bought our first home. We made the decision to homeschool Jonathan, as public school had proven a poor match for our highly sensitive, academically gifted son. Courtney attended a special school for the disabled. Jerry finally decided to become Catholic and came into the Church at Easter Vigil in 1999. As a couple, we continued to struggle to accept each other, and we still tried to mask our pain with our addictions.

Jonathan continued to show signs of distress over how to be a typical kid whose life included an atypical sibling. Courtney was still having seizures, still cortically blind, and still in a wheelchair. Her overall medical condition continued to decline. She struggled to swallow without aspirating food into her lungs. At seven, she weighed only thirty-two pounds instead of the average of nearly fifty pounds. She was diagnosed with "failure to thrive," so we opted to have a gastrostomy tube (G-tube) surgically placed to assist her feeding. She started attending a new school for the profoundly disabled but struggled to make any developmental progress. She could not break through the development window of a nine-month-old child. Every week was filled with doctor visits, rigidly scheduled feedings, and seizures, but that didn't dampen her spirit. She was feisty with her curly blond hair and cornflower blue eyes. She loved music and would get excited when Garth Brooks came on the radio. She was content most days, and for that I was grateful.

Homeschooling Jonathan brought a glimmer of hope. It gave him the individual attention that he desperately missed and brought us a bit closer as a family. For that, I was willing to do anything, even teach long division. Time would tell if it was a good decision or not.

HOPE FOR A MIRACLE

Through another homeschool family, we found out about the Knights of Malta and their annual healing pilgrimage to Lourdes, France. After many years and so many disappointments, Jerry and I were growing tired of running after new treatments and trying new medications that didn't work. We had arrived at the conclusion that if our daughter were to be healed, it would only be by a miracle of God.

Amazingly, the Knights of Malta made it possible for Jerry and me to travel with Courtney on the pilgrimage to Lourdes. The trip was beyond anything we could have imagined. Six million people visit Lourdes each year, eighty thousand of them to seek healing from their illnesses and afflictions. Numerous miracles have been attributed to bathing in the spring discovered by St. Bernadette during her visions of the Blessed Virgin Mary in 1858.

The sun was shining the day we took Courtney into the healing baths. Jerry and I shared a sense of hope that God was moving mountains and that Courtney would soon be returned to health. Our daughter was carried to the grotto on a stretcher. Jerry was ushered to the men's side of the baths. As the two of us entered the small stone room for women and children, four women stood ready to assist me in preparing Courtney to enter the waters.

A French woman asked me what our daughter's "ailments" were. She began to touch Courtney's body with a little statue of the Blessed Mother that was about five inches long. I told her that Courtney had seizures and could not walk or speak or see. Praying for Our Lady's intercession, the woman moved to place the statue next to our daughter's head.

As the woman passed the statue over Courtney's head, my daughter did something unique in her life: she grabbed hold of the statue of Mary. She had never before intentionally reached for or held anything other than her bottle, and I never again saw her perform such an action after that day. When I stepped forward to pry it from her hand, Courtney moved the statue to place it over her heart. Then she slowly brought down her other fisted hand and placed it on top of the first, firmly holding the statue.

I stared in amazement at my blind, nonverbal, profoundly disabled daughter clutching that tiny statue of Mary. The entire time she was in the water, Courtney never moved her arms; Mary stayed right near my daughter's heart.

A WORD IN THE WATERS

Courtney was lifted out of the water and laid back onto the stretcher. Suddenly, it was my turn. I moved quickly. Reciting the prayer I had practiced for this moment, I stepped into the water—and stopped abruptly. I have never in my lifetime felt anything as frigid as that water. It was ice cold! I was frozen in place like a holy popsicle. For a moment everything became very foggy to me. Then I heard a young girl's voice say a single word: "Acceptance." I shook my head and looked around. Surely, I had heard one of the women volunteers praying for me. But the women's heads were bowed in silent prayer. The only young girl in the room was Courtney.

One of the attendants asked what my prayer was. I replied, "Acceptance." It was all I could think to say in the moment, though I didn't have the faintest idea what it meant. The women dunked me backward into the water and helped me out. Dressing myself, I walked over to my daughter, who was still laid out on the stretcher. She was very happy and was humming softly, ready to go back into her wheelchair. But I wanted to see if the miraculous healing we had hoped and prayed for had occurred.

I lifted Courtney to her feet, and she began to laugh. I placed her feet on the ground and tried to let go. She laughed again and started to sink to her bum. Realizing that she was not going to stand, I scooped her up and whispered into her ear how much I loved her—whether she could walk or not.

NO COINCIDENCE

Apparently, God wanted my daughter to be as she was, and my job was to *accept* it. I swallowed my disappointment and accepted God's provision of grace. He had placed the word *acceptance* in my heart; this *must* be what he meant.

I looked up when we came out of the baths, and the first person I saw was Jerry, wearing a huge smile on his face. As he looked at Courtney sitting in her wheelchair, a single tear slipped down his face. I wheeled Courtney over to him, wrapped my arms around him, held him tightly, and whispered my love in his ear. I didn't understand God's exact plan right then, but a peace settled over me, and that was enough.

Jerry knelt down and pulled Courtney into his arms. She giggled and called out loudly. Jerry kissed her curly head, and we headed over to the grotto for Mass with our pilgrimage group. When the bells rang as the priest held up Our Lord at the consecration, Courtney laughed and started humming loudly. I looked over, meaning to hush her, but stopped when I saw the joy written all over her face. She was looking at the altar as though she could see it. I felt like I was watching a private conversation between Courtney and God. It took my breath away.

After Mass, Jerry and I pushed Courtney up the hill for lunch. I poured out my heart, telling him everything that had happened with Courtney in the water. Then Jerry dropped a bombshell on me: he had gone into the baths as well, and he too had heard a young girl's voice say "acceptance" as he stepped into the water.

This was no coincidence. "What does it mean, Jerry? What do we do now?" I asked.

Laying out the battle plan, Jerry replied, "We love our daughter, and we live our life. God will take care of the rest."

GRACE UPON GRACE

When we shared what had happened in the water with our fellow pilgrims, no one seemed surprised. One of the Knights of Malta told us to get ready because many miracles that began in Lourdes came to full fruition later. He said it was just the beginning. I believed him. One priest asked if Courtney was going to receive her First Communion since she was seven years old, the typical age for first reception of Eucharist at our parish. I informed him that there was no way to catechize her and no way to know what she understood and what she did not. He simply laughed and told me that Courtney had showed us she knew exactly where she was in the grotto and how much she loved Jesus and his mother by what she did in the water. So two days later in Lourdes, France, wearing a white dress and veil given to us by our sponsors, my beautiful daughter received Our Lord in the Eucharist for the first time.

Although Courtney was not healed, we had received a miracle. Courtney had received Holy Communion. Such an unexpected gift! Her countenance changed, and she was calmer and seemed at peace. It's hard to explain when your child is nonverbal, but she just seemed happy, as if she knew that everything would be okay. We had received God's grace with new openness and understanding. We went home changed parents filled with peace, hope, and even joy. Jerry and I still struggled with the word *acceptance* and wondered aloud to each other if there was something more that we had missed. Most days, though, our attention was focused on caring for Courtney. When the seizures came, I simply prayed for the grace to accept whatever the remainder of the day would hold. This time, I let go of control and did not take it back.

PATH TO PEACE

When we offer up a situation to God and accept (rather than resign ourselves to) the outcome he provides, the burdens become easier. I promise. Why? Because we are cooperating with the God who loves us while we're walking through the yuckiness. Being with him gives us a sense of peace, and this peace makes it possible for us to find joy. When we invest in our relationship with the Lord, it pays out through his love and peace. His generosity cannot be outdone.

Now this may sound crazy because accepting reality and offering up a situation to God doesn't stop the suffering or make the problems go away. We are not wired for acceptance, to be sure. We *want* a pill, a quick fix, a silver bullet to make things all better instantly. But what we really *need* is to hand the entire mess over to God and always, always remember that "all things work for good for those who love God, who are called according to his purpose" (Rom 8:28).

This surrender of our pain and suffering, or just our plain old difficulties dealing with daily life, is probably the hardest part of acceptance. Moving forward without having any sense of what the outcome will be requires a huge amount of trust. There is an order to this, however: Faith leads to trust. Trust leads to acceptance. Acceptance leads to surrender. Surrender leads to peace. Acceptance allows us to be who we are and allows God to be who he is.

Acceptance is where healing begins. Life didn't get any easier for us. It did, however, become richer and more filled with love and meaning. This shift can happen only when you're ready to hear God's truth and move beyond your desire and need to fix the situation. If you wallow in the misery, you allow no room for the joy God has for you. And there is joy, even in the difficult times.

PUTTING THE PIECES TOGETHER

Four years passed, and we found ourselves in another hospital waiting room as Courtney underwent a procedure to assist her with seizure control. Usually I had a sense of peace about medical procedures, but this time felt different. I grabbed my

notepad and Bible out of my bag, opened to Psalm 107, took a
deep breath, and read:

> O give thanks to the LORD, for he is good;
>> for his steadfast love endures forever. . . .
> Some went down to the sea in ships,
>> doing business on the mighty waters;
> they saw the deeds of the LORD,
>> his wondrous works in the deep.
> For he commanded and raised the stormy wind,
>> which lifted up the waves of the sea.
> They mounted up to heaven, they went down to the depths;
>> their courage melted away in their calamity;
> they reeled and staggered like drunkards,
>> and were at their wits' end.
> Then they cried to the LORD in their trouble,
>> and he brought them out from their distress;
> he made the storm be still,
>> and the waves of the sea were hushed.
> Then they were glad because they had quiet,
>> and he brought them to their desired haven.
> Let them thank the LORD for his steadfast love,
>> for his wonderful works to humankind.
> Let them extol him in the congregation of the people,
>> and praise him in the assembly of the elders.
>> (vv. 1, 23–32, NRSV)

It was my father's favorite psalm, one he had highlighted in
his Breviary. He had gone home to the Lord three years earlier,
and in that moment, I missed him terribly. When we returned
from Lourdes, Dad had told us that God wasn't done. When we
mentioned our confusion in hearing the word *acceptance*, he had
told us to be patient, "to wait for the answer." I closed my eyes
and asked my dad to be with Courtney, so that she wouldn't be

afraid. Suddenly, I felt someone squeeze my shoulder just like Dad used to do.

I opened my eyes and looked around the room. Jerry was reading his book quietly. We were the only ones sitting on our side of the waiting room. I shook my head and smiled. *Daddy, you're here. . . . I really miss you. . . . Why do I feel so unsettled, Dad? Help me, please. . . . Help me figure it out.*

I read the psalm again and then opened my notepad and reread some of the notes I had taken at the women's retreat I had attended the weekend before. I came across my notes from the priest's last talk about redemptive suffering and healing:

> First, there are miraculous healings, times when God intervenes and a person is healed of an ailment in a way the medical establishment is unable to explain. Second, there is healing after a time of suffering, for example, someone who is declared cancer-free after undergoing chemo. Third, there is an acceptance of the suffering with the knowledge that there will be no healing here on earth but only when we see the face of God.

I read that last sentence again . . . then again . . . and again. My heart started to beat faster. *Acceptance.*

I grabbed Jerry's hand and told him to read my notes. He did, then looked up and shook his head. "What am I missing?"

"What are *we* missing? I am amazed at God's patience with fools like us. Remember when we were in Lourdes? Courtney went into the water first; then we followed."

He nodded.

"Remember the word that was given to both of us at the same time?"

"Acceptance."

HER VOICE

I felt excited, like a TV detective who had just solved the case. "Jerry, what two prayers have we always prayed for Courtney?" I asked.

"That we would hear her voice and that we would be with her when she died," he answered, almost indignantly.

"Read it again," I commanded, pointing to the notepad. I watched his eyes get bigger as he read.

"You see it too," I said, smiling. Lourdes was the only time we had been completely open to God's voice. We had prayed for a miracle, and we had had hundreds of people interceding for us. Now, we finally realized that it was our daughter's voice we had heard. She couldn't speak in a language the world understands; she needed help telling us. God had let us hear her voice.

"She knows, Jerry. Courtney knows and accepts that there won't be any healing here. How else can you explain everything that has happened? Her peaceful nature, the absolute joy she exudes to everyone around her, the way she draws people to her, the way her witness of peace and acceptance of circumstance brings people to their knees in prayerful support. We've seen it time and time again when I've asked people to pray for her. Remember last night after Mass, when Father gathered some parishioners to pray over her because she was having surgery today? That doesn't just happen. Courtney inspires people to pray. Somewhere along the way, she said yes to God, and she needed us to know that it's okay. Courtney has accepted her cross. Remember when the Knight of Malta told us that miracles start in Lourdes, and it may take time for us to fully understand what has happened? Four years, babe. It took four!"

His mouth was opening and closing like a fish's. "That's why your dad said, 'Be patient.' We couldn't see it all yet. He understood."

"Of course he did. Dad did the same thing. He said yes to God knowing that his healing from cancer would only come from Our Lord. I bet you that's what he whispered to her that last day when he said goodbye. Holy cow, no one is going to believe us. No one. This is just crazy, but I know in my soul that this is what acceptance means, what it really means for us and for our family."

In that moment, we were able to see God's plan. At the time, it seemed as if *everything* changed; in reality, *we* were what changed. Jerry and I spent the next ninety minutes in prayer, right there in the hospital. We said the Rosary, read scripture together, and asked God for clarification. We now knew that we had heard the sound of our daughter's yes to God. We had a mission, but so did she. She would travel the way of the cross she had accepted. We would love her and take care of her needs. We would also be Courtney's hands and feet and her voice when she needed to be heard. Our family would make the journey of faith together and help her tell the story of God's mercy and love. I had no idea what that would look like practically, but I knew that living our life boldly and without fear would be a game changer.

UNPACKING THE GIFT

Life is lived differently when we learn to accept that we cannot change our circumstances and still choose to hope. While our family's day-to-day life did not change after that day in the hospital, we experienced it very differently. Our attitudes and the way we handled the stress were completely transformed by grace.

We had been walking in fear and grief for so long that freedom and joy felt odd and uncomfortable. But whenever we began to question what we had discerned, we got on our knees and surrendered that fear and questioning again. Time after time, we reclaimed our peace and continued to live openly with our daughter. We no longer hid in fear of her seizures and difficult care or worried about what others would think or say. Instead, we shared her journey with anyone who would listen.

Are you ready to give your difficulty, pain, and suffering to God? Do not hesitate to hand it over, my friend. I cannot implore you enough to just lay it down and allow God to carry that burden for you.

How have the power and grace of God appeared to you? Are you still unpacking something God has revealed to you? It took four years for us to completely unlock what happened in Lourdes. Thankfully, God is infinitely patient, faithful, and generous with his wisdom and understanding. Ask him into the confusion and pain, and allow him to shine the light of his love on you. Allow God to do for you what you cannot do for yourself. He is waiting to bring healing and to restore your hope.

JOHN 8:32

And you will know the truth, and the truth will set you free.

CHAPTER SEVEN

SACRIFICE AND SELF-GIFT

Our culture is inundated with fairy tales about finding true love and seeking our own personal happily-ever-after. Isn't that what we all want in life—to be loved without condition? To be seen and heard and accepted for who we are? (Note how we don't usually daydream about finding the person we will love without limit. Usually, it's all about lining up the poor sucker who will love us.)

But what are the *greatest* love stories in the world? Invariably, they involve someone who is willing to sacrifice and another who is willing to receive that offer of self-gift. In the greatest love story ever, God offers us his Son, Jesus, who freely sacrifices himself that we may know how much we are loved. The Cross is how we get to our eternal happily-ever-after.

In marriage, husbands and wives are called to offer themselves in service and sacrifice to their spouses—to place the needs of the other above their own. Because we are human, we are not always going to get that right. We are going to be selfish. We are going to fail, and in that failure, we are going to wound the other, sometimes deeply. We hurt the people closest to us because we trust that they won't leave. But they often do leave—if not physically, then emotionally or spiritually. As our hearts become hardened toward each other, we begin to build walls that prevent us from fully entering into the sacrifice of self-gift.

FORGIVENESS

However, there comes a moment when you recognize that carrying the weight of unforgiveness is preventing you from fully loving and fully receiving love. In that moment a choice must be made between staying in the darkness of woundedness and fear and making the self-sacrifice of choosing to forgive. We are called to be brave in the scared and love without condition.

Forgiveness is all about love. Forgiveness is a gift to the one who forgives, not just to the one who is forgiven. It's a relief to let go of the rancor and bitterness that push out all the good that we are supposed to be doing with our lives. Most of us wait for some healing to occur before we are willing to forgive. But that's inside-out and backwards. The act of forgiveness allows that healing to actually take place. In time, and if God wills it, he can redeem our hurt and use its footprint for a new beginning.

Jerry and I spent many years living in fear that one of us would leave the other. Neither of us felt worthy of true and unconditional love. Both of us felt we had made too many mistakes for anyone to forgive. We had hardened our hearts and were living behind walls of self-preservation. We were lost and had no idea how to find our way back to one another. We had not yet accepted that we were each other's path to God. If we could not forgive each other, then how could we hope that God would forgive us?

It was difficult to admit that all we were doing was piling hurt upon each other, and that this hurt was just creating more problems. By allowing distortion of our intimacy in the bedroom, we had pushed God out of almost every aspect of our lives. We went to Mass regularly, but out of duty and not because we truly wanted to be there. We were living like children in fear of a father's wrath.

CHANGE OVER TIME

We returned from Lourdes changed people. The conversion that began in the healing waters started to renew and refresh the intimacy within our marriage. In our attempts to break bad habits and distorted thinking, however, we needed to learn patience and gentleness both toward each other and toward ourselves.

We knew that God had spoken to us, that we had experienced him as we never had before. Still, God can't heal what you won't give him, so we slowly began to hand over our deeply wounded marriage to him, one hurt at a time. Over the course of the next few years, we went to a Marriage Encounter, Jerry signed up for a men's retreat, and I started attending Overeaters Anonymous meetings. We slowly surrendered our addictions and continued to build upon the acceptance and hope we discovered in Lourdes.

We strove, as a couple, to find our way back to each other. We stopped viewing porn and made a concerted effort to stop digging the hole of our emotional avoidance deeper. We began to take baby steps toward renewing our marriage. We knew it was going to be a very long process, but we had hope again. There was a lightness to our relationship that had not been there since we were dating. Things were not perfect, and we still fell into sin from time to time, but we were determined to stay the course. We had made a commitment to our children not to quit and not to leave each other. Now we had to do the hard work necessary to keep our family together. We wanted to be healed and whole once more.

MENTORS WANTED

One fall afternoon in 2007, shortly after Courtney's fifteenth birthday, our pastor, Fr. B., approached us with an idea. He wanted to start a parish marriage ministry in which seasoned couples would walk alongside engaged couples preparing for marriage. The couples would meet once a month for a meal in the sponsoring couple's home. The idea was to foster a mentorship and open conversation about marriage and the realities that exist in that very complicated covenant. Fr. B. asked if we would consider being one of the mentor couples. He also wanted us to become qualified Natural Family Planning instructors.

Jerry and I looked at each other and started laughing (probably not the response our pastor expected). Then my hubby, in his marvelously snarky manner, gave his response: "Seasoned? Is that the same thing as old? Seriously, if you're looking to the two of us to provide adult supervision to engaged couples, you must be crazy. You have got to be kidding me. Father, if I wrote my autobiography, the title would be *Sometimes, Your Life Is an Example of What Not to Do*."

But Fr. B. just smiled and reassured us that he knew all about our history and what we were still working through. He said, "You fell, but you got up time and time again. You love each other, and you have not given up on your marriage. I want couples who have been through the wringer and have chosen to forgive. That's the beauty of this covenant you and Mary share. You chose forgiveness instead of bitterness. Hope instead of hate."

I just chuckled; knowing there was no way that Jerry would agree to do such a thing, I told him that I would happily accept whatever he chose to do. I did this very secure in the knowledge that he would be way too uncomfortable to mentor engaged couples.

You can stop laughing now. Yes, you are correct, and I was quite wrong. Jerry agreed to it all. I could not have been more shocked. *Well*, I thought apprehensively, *now what have we gotten ourselves into? What could we tell young couples about marriage, chastity, and forgiveness?* We were still working through all these things ourselves.

RETRAINED

So off we went to the weeklong training required for mentor couples. Since we were not comfortable leaving Courtney that long, we convinced my mother to come along and assist us with her care while we were in class. Jonathan stayed behind, thrilled to spend the week with his best friend. We packed our bags, loaded the wheelchair van, and headed north, totally unsure what to expect.

First up was Christopher West's intense Theology of the Body seminar in Lima, Pennsylvania. We arrived on a Sunday afternoon in late September and were greeted with such humility and grace. Christopher and his team didn't blink twice as we wheeled Courtney into the retreat house. They were very kind to assist us with special accommodations, making the week as easy as possible for my mom and Courtney so that Jerry and I could fully enter into the teaching. They recognized and respected the dignity of our daughter in a way I had not witnessed before. It was beautiful to watch them all speaking to her as if nothing was awry, seeing her as fully capable, and treating her with such kindness. It allowed Jerry and me to be at ease so we could concentrate on what was in front of us.

The program was tough. The first two days left us reeling; there was just so much to take in. The presentations helped us slowly come to understand the beauty of our bodies' language and the power with which they speak to one another within the marital embrace.

It was painful, though, to fully realize how badly we had stumbled in our marriage. The staggering statistics presented on the pervasiveness of porn and the stories that revealed its objectification of the individual and the damage it inflicts on the marriage union were sobering to say the least. Jerry and I were completely overwhelmed as we recognized the impact our choices had made on our marriage as well as on our individual identities as sexual beings. By Wednesday morning, we were quiet with one another. As we settled in for another day's lecture, I worried that we might not be able to overcome the lingering legacy of our shared sin.

Christopher began the day with an explanation of chastity within marriage and the damage that objectifying one's spouse can do to the intimate dance of the marital embrace. We knew the truth of that firsthand. What we had not yet discovered was that the life-giving love of sexual union also had the power to heal our hearts of their deepest wounds. We knew that love is lost when people use each other and that what remains is lust. Eventually, lust destroys the heart and changes the most intimate of marital acts into a source of death rather than a source of life.

The guilt and shame we felt were very real. We heard in the lecture the hard truth that my husband had treated me as a prostitute, and I knew that I had willingly allowed it. I looked at Jerry, but he refused to make eye contact with me. I was desperate for him to know that he did not bear full responsibility for what had transpired in our marriage bed. There are three in a marriage, but we had together thrown God out years before. In those three days, we recognized the enormity of that choice.

NO TURNING BACK

Yes, we had made great strides in the last few years, but hearing plainly, without emotional attachment, the impact our choices had had on our intimate life was difficult. It cut my husband and me to the quick. When Confession was offered at the break, we were the first in line. We were finally ready to surrender our marriage completely and totally to the restorative grace and mercy of God.

An hour later, we stood alone on the back deck of the retreat house. The crisp breeze rustled the leaves in the trees. Neither of us said a word. We just stood in peace, taking in the immensity of finally being free from those sins. Jerry took my hand and spoke quietly: "I made you feel like a prostitute, didn't I? I am so very sorry, Mary. I didn't realize what a toll my own wounds would have on you, our marriage, or our family. Will you please forgive me?"

I turned to him with tears in my eyes, gave him my forgiveness, and then asked for his. As I looked into my husband's eyes, all I saw was freedom and grace. I was overcome with joy and gratitude for God's faithfulness and mercy. He was restoring our marriage, and I knew that when we left that retreat house, our life together would be a source of joy.

We renewed our wedding vows that fall day, just Jerry and I, surrounded by the beauty of God's creation. There would be no turning back for either of us. Yes, there would be temptations for sure, but that day we knew that God had healed and redeemed our marriage bed, and we vowed never to defile it again.

HOPE FOR REDEMPTION

When you confuse selfishness with sacrifice, everyone loses. To heal our marriage, we had to ask God's forgiveness as well as forgiveness from each other. God taught us that there is always hope for redemption, that no sin committed is beyond forgiveness, and that no one is beyond salvation. God's grace and mercy cover all.

Jerry and I went on to become marriage mentors and, after we were trained, taught the symptothermal method of Natural Family Planning for three years. We were able to set aside our own embarrassment about my tubal ligation and our use of pornography and share our journey with engaged couples openly and honestly. We did so because we knew that there were many couples who needed to hear about God's generosity with us. The lessons we learned in the first two decades of our marriage were hard ones, and we were grateful to have made it through such difficulties. Not everyone does.

By choosing radical forgiveness, Jerry and I have been able to receive ongoing grace from God. We did not allow our sinful past to be brought up during an argument or disagreement in order for one spouse to gain the upper hand by hurting the other. Our marriage continued to grow stronger. Since our time in Pennsylvania, we have enjoyed a deeper intimacy than we ever thought possible. Remember how earlier I said that life was too much for one person to handle? How I didn't mention a couple? Well, we were finally able to reestablish our relationship, working as a team to shore up the foundations of our marriage and family. Jerry's attitude toward me and our intimacy had completely changed for the better. I was excited to see where God was going to take us.

IT TAKES TIME

Our healing did not happen overnight; we had to commit again and again to persevering through the doubt and the fear. We had to choose forgiveness daily. As time passes, the gift of God's redemption of our marriage and the gentleness we show one another continues to bear fruit. With each choice to forgive or ask for forgiveness, God's blessings pour forth and we are amazed by his steadfast love.

Do you expect God's grace to produce immediate results? They say time heals all wounds. I'm not sure I believe that, but I do know that time can soften some blows. When you make a decision to forgive, be prepared for Satan to do everything in his power to thwart your efforts. Forgiving someone who has deeply hurt you will be difficult. In the end, however, the freedom you receive from letting go of that hurt restores and redeems. That freedom is a channel of God's unlimited grace and mercy. Holding on to the offense and the anger ultimately hurts only you.

Have you settled for less than true love? I understand what it feels like to stand in abject loneliness and fear that you will never be loved for who you truly are. Do not lose hope, my friend. Be gentle toward yourself, and walk in the knowledge that God uses *all* things—even the worst things! We all fall short, and sometimes it takes a decade (or two) to turn the ship around or get back on the right track. But do not quit. God walks beside you, encouraging you to enter more deeply into a loving relationship with him.

Be brave, friend. You have nothing to fear. Ask God into your humiliation and sorrow. By doing so, you allow his healing grace and mercy to flow freely and guide you from selfishness toward self-gift.

ROMANS 3:23-25

All have sinned and are deprived of the glory of God. They are justified freely by his grace through the redemption in Christ Jesus, whom God set forth as an expiation, through faith, by his blood, to prove his righteousness because of the forgiveness of sins previously committed.

CHAPTER EIGHT

MERCY IN THE MESS

Life is messy. Even if you're a neat freak and your spice rack is organized alphabetically, I'll bet your life is still messy. You may do a great job keeping your mess hidden in a closet, the basement, or the garage—but it's there.

Some of our messes are ones we've made for ourselves. Some are made for us by other people. And then there are those messes that seem to fall from the sky like droppings from a flock of geese. Duck and cover!

Three of the greatest lies Satan routinely whispers into our hearts are (1) you deserve pain and suffering; (2) you can successfully avoid pain and suffering; and (3) God doesn't care. Let's take those on one at a time.

SATAN'S FIRST LIE: YOU DESERVE IT

First, terrible misfortune isn't always the natural consequence of a choice we made. It can happen to anyone and without warning. We don't have to do anything to deserve it. Trust me, pain has a way of finding us. But whether it affects us directly or someone we love, suffering can change a person's personality and belief system. When the pain is intense or lasts over a prolonged period of time, we are tempted to lose hope or, even worse, our faith.

We are also tempted to find someone to blame. More often than not, the person in the mirror takes the rap.

Although our faith teaches us that suffering can have meaning, physical, emotional, and interpersonal pain can overwhelm us. That's when we forget that there's a divine purpose in everything. Most of us don't care much about the purpose of the suffering we undergo; we just want it to stop.

SATAN'S SECOND LIE: YOU CAN AVOID IT

Another common coping mechanism posed by Satan is what I call the running away program. When we don't want to deal with a mess, we just pretend we don't have one. We numb ourselves with addictions or diversions. Chocolate ice cream and Netflix, anyone? Maybe we don't feel that we have the faith or physical strength to deal with the pain, so we don't. Or maybe we think that we should have been able to avoid suffering in the first place, so we take the better-late-than-never approach.

We are built with a fight-or-flight instinct. I think the flight side of the equation includes avoidance. We hide and hope it will all just disappear. The physical and emotional pain feels like too much to bear. Although we were never meant to bear them alone, we choose to hide our messes from others and from God. We forget about who made us, who loves us, and who is there to help us.

SATAN'S THIRD LIE: GOD DOESN'T CARE

In the midst of struggle, it's very easy to fall into a pattern of self-pity. Usually, it's because the loudest voice in our head wins. Desperation shouts Satan's third lie, the false conclusion that no one—not even God—cares about what is happening to us. And when we begin to believe that we, or our situation, can never change, we've begun the descent into hopelessness. That can leave us feeling not only helpless but also unworthy of being helped.

NOT AS PLANNED

So how do we see through these three lies? We must accept our suffering, even embrace it, and ask God into the depths of our experience. That answer is easy to speak yet hard to live.

We encountered suffering not only in our marriage and in what caring for Courtney required of us but also with our son, Jonathan, as he headed off to college in the fall of 2008. He had excelled in the homeschool environment from second grade through high school graduation. With co-op classes and a tutor or two, homeschooling gave our son the one-on-one attention he had been craving as well as sufficient academic challenge to keep his attention and focus. He was a straight-A student through the majority of high school. Nevertheless, he was not the most organized or self-motivated individual. I was concerned. And, as tends to happen in our family, nothing went as planned.

Jonathan was excited to be living on his own, but he struggled with every aspect of college life. Living with strangers, the academic rigor of an honors college program that required self-motivation and organization, as well as the loneliness from being four states away from family: they were not what he had expected. After three difficult semesters, Jerry and I felt it was best for Jonathan to come home.

We soon discovered that our son barely resembled the young man we'd sent to college. He was bitter and angry, and we couldn't understand why. His short temper and irate outbursts set off alarm bells. He had always been a sensitive and empathetic young man with a strong sense of justice, but he returned broken. Jerry and I quickly came to understand that our son was in deep emotional trouble, and we were way out of our league to do anything about it. We needed help.

We sought counsel from our dear friends and our pastor, and we prayed for the wisdom of Solomon to do the right thing for him. Jonathan agreed to see a psychiatrist, and this was truly a grace. Because this particular doctor loved movies and science fiction, he was immediately able to relate to Jonathan in a way that enabled Jonathan to lower his emotional wall. Slowly but surely, he helped Jonathan peel away the layers of his hurt and trauma. Some startling truths were revealed. The psychiatrist diagnosed Jonathan with severe depression and anxiety. He also told us that our son suffered from post-traumatic stress disorder (PTSD) as a result of his sister's seizures.

As we began to unpack the doctor's findings, we learned about two specific traumatic events in his life of which Jerry and I had been completely unaware. Both had happened when he was in high school. On two occasions when I had left him with Courtney while I went to the grocery store, Courtney had seized and, in both cases, stopped breathing for a few seconds. These frightening moments had traumatized Jonathan. He felt responsible to care for his sister but believed he had failed. Because he wanted to protect us, he had never shared these experiences with us.

HEARTBROKEN

I was devastated by these disclosures. In my mind, God had betrayed Jonathan by allowing him to go through depression, anxiety, and PTSD. It was so unfair. Didn't our family have enough to deal with? Wasn't Jonathan's life hard enough?

Terrified for my son's well-being, I allowed my imagination to drag me down roads I didn't want to travel. My own anxiety spiraled out of control. I was a pro at ER visits, but neither Jerry nor I had any experience with mental illness. We were flying blind, and it wasn't pretty. It wasn't long until I struggled with my own mental health. I was one big ball of worry. I wasn't sleeping and spent most days railing at God and struggling with guilt. Just as when he was in preschool, I felt I was responsible for Jonathan's problems.

Three months into intensive therapy, Jonathan asked Jerry and me to join him for one session with his psychiatrist, Dr. Joe. I was nervous, having no idea what to expect. Jonathan would not make eye contact with me as we took our seats. Dr. Joe opened with a prayer. Then he told us that Jonathan had things he needed to say and asked that we refrain from responding or reacting in any way until he was finished. We agreed.

In the next two minutes, the gates of Jonathan's heart opened, and his pain came flooding out. Jonathan revealed his belief that we did not love him as much as we loved Courtney. We always set him and his needs aside. He would never be able to measure up to how perfect we were and how we never made mistakes. He was angry that he had to carry the burden of being Courtney's only sibling. The worst moment was when he expressed guilt over being the surviving sibling, even though Courtney was still alive. He was the stronger of the two; he felt that the disability should have been his, not Courtney's.

SHARING THE PAIN

As Jonathan spoke honestly, Jerry and I absorbed his pain. We tried not to react, but neither Jerry nor I could stop our tears. Our beautiful son felt abandoned by his parents and, due to our neglect, had experienced great trauma. Jonathan ended in tears.

He told us that he loved us nonetheless and admitted that he wanted to be loved in return. He felt he deserved at least that.

I couldn't breathe. I saw that I had consistently placed Courtney's needs ahead of Jonathan's. By doing so, I had created a vacuum of doubt in my son that his parents loved him equally. This caused Jonathan to feel that he was not being heard and that his needs would not be met. And we hadn't realized how badly he had been hurt.

Suddenly, I was right back in that bedroom with four-year-old Jonathan, asking God to help me love him as much as I loved Courtney. Yet again, it was made clear to me that I had failed to meet his needs. I felt crushed. I looked to the doctor for instruction, and he indicated that we could now speak.

My husband and I leaned forward and took turns asking for Jonathan's forgiveness for the things we did and didn't do that made him feel abandoned and set aside. We assured him of our love and told him how proud we were of him. We told him that God had a plan for his life too, and we expressed how honored we were to be his parents. Sitting with all the pain and figuring out how to let it go was going to be his greatest battle.

By the end of the session we were all crying and holding each other. Jerry prayed over Jonathan and asked the Holy Spirit to be with each of us as we walked toward healing and restoration as a family. The doctor then gave us detailed instructions for daily communication to assist Jonathan as he continued to work through the pain.

ONE MORE THING

At the end of the session, Jonathan brought up one last wound. He stated in total seriousness that I had not hugged him enough. Now Jonathan is a big guy, six feet two and built like a linebacker. This was not what we expected to hear after all the big feels we had just experienced. Jerry and I totally cracked up—clearly not the reaction Jonathan or Dr. Joe was expecting. I stopped laughing long enough to say, "Dude, you haven't wanted me to hug you in public since you were nine years old. I've tried. Somehow I always embarrass you."

"Well, I know, Mom," he answered, looking sheepishly at me. "But now I think I wouldn't mind it so much."

We solved that little problem right then and there with the first Lenaburg family bear hug in over a decade. My new rule was that any mom hug required at least one minute. Since then, I insist on a hug after Jonathan gets home from work every day— after he's showered, of course. Getting bear-hugged by a sweaty linebacker is not a good thing. Even if he is your son.

That day, as hard as it was to hear the truth and to bear witness to my son's suffering, was the first day of a new family dialogue, bear hugs included, that would bring healing.

Six months later, we sat at the kitchen table and Jonathan shared a recent counseling session; he said something profound without using a single SAT word. "Mom," he said, "thanks for finding Dr. Joe for me. It's really helping. He's restored my faith that everything is going to be okay. God's got this, Mom. It's his to carry. It will be okay."

His voice was calm and self-assured, with no doubt. Jonathan had surrendered. He had come to his own place of simple trust and faith in God. He knew everything was in God's hands.

Since the day we confronted the truth together, Jonathan has made steady progress in dealing with his emotions and trauma and is doing fabulously well. As we like to tell him, he has definitely learned to "adult." He is an assistant manager at the store where he works and, more importantly, a young man who loves God. We could not be prouder of our son and how he has risen from the ashes of his own pain and despair to live a faith-filled life, which, he hopes, may one day include a family of his own. (His mother hopes so, too!)

REDEEMING LOVE

Trying to avoid pain led to a life of addiction for Jerry and me and to our son's isolation and depression. When our world is rocked by trauma and we cannot see our life apart from it, we feel as though our feet are stuck in cement. First, we must exercise an act of the will to trust the Father, a deliberate choice to invite him into the mess. Second, we must make an act of faith to be able to see the trauma of our lives as God sees it. And third, we must choose to be generous, to give our pain to God in order to join it to the Cross.

That is how we can become part of God's redeeming love. When our family finally embraced our daily struggles and pain, they became more than just suffering. They became sacrifices. It was then that each of us was given the grace to heal and find wholeness.

Through Jonathan, God reminded me, *again*, that there is no way around suffering: we must walk through it. Hugging may help, but it doesn't solve everything. If we can't escape pain or fix it, we must embrace it. When we do, God reveals hidden gifts, blessings, and hope.

We will have hardships in this world, but Jesus came into the world to *enter into* the depths of our lives—the emptiness, abandonment, betrayal, loneliness, and physical pain—for the sole purpose of transforming us. Why would the Creator of the world do this for us? To redeem us. When we embrace our suffering, everything changes.

BRAVE IN THE SCARED

Being brave in the scared means facing the hard challenges that we can't escape no matter how hard we try. Is there any suffering you are still trying to avoid? Oh, friend, learn from my experiences and be brave. Enter into that suffering, and walk through it. Hold your head high knowing that the lessons God wishes to impart are worth it and that he will carry you through. You will not forget the truths you learn while walking through your trials. Healing and hope live in fiery moments of grace.

Overcoming despair means finding hope, especially in the Cross. God is there, friends. He is there in the big and the small, in the hurt and the joy, in the trial and the triumph. Ask Jesus into your heart, and then wait to see how he chooses to restore you. You will not be disappointed.

God has laced his mercy and redemption through my life like ivy looping around a great tower, twisting and turning to fill in the gaps in the stonework. He has been faithful and generous to me, and his wisdom and grace abound day after day. When I fall (and yes, I still fall), he is there to scoop me up, hold me close, and assure me that he will never abandon me. He will do the same for you.

Are you able to accept pain and disappointment? Is there something you've done everything in your power to avoid? How has the work of God, the glory of God, been revealed in your life? Allow God to walk with you, friend. If you do, he will show you his mercy in the middle of your mess.

JOHN 9:2-3

His disciples asked him, "Rabbi, who sinned, this man or his parents, that he was born blind?" Jesus answered, "Neither he nor his parents sinned; it is so that the works of God might be made visible through him."

CHAPTER NINE

WHO YOU REALLY ARE

Who am I? Why am I here? What is my purpose? These are the most basic questions we ask ourselves throughout life. The challenge is that our identity and self-worth can become wrapped up in what we *do* instead of who God says we *are*. Our society, of course, has reinforced this idea by measuring people's success or worth in life by the things they own or the things they've accomplished. When we don't achieve that bank-balance or résumé success, it's easy for us to feel as if we don't measure up or are even unworthy of love.

We are so steeped in society's notion of expectations and achievements that we never stop to think that there is truly *nothing* we can do to earn God's love—or to lose it. No matter what we do or don't do, God sees us as valuable and lovable. God's love is simply present to us and freely given every day. It is our choice, however, whether to accept his love. When we do, we become more who he intended us to be, and this is where our true happiness lies.

Still, we can lose ourselves. This can happen when we suffer a different loss, such as the loss of a job or salary, the ending of a marriage, or a failure to achieve a dream or goal that we set for ourselves. We have placed so much value on what we do, we forget that it has no impact on how much God loves us. It's also easy to lose sight of who we are when we become caretakers for others or are simultaneously helping aging parents while raising our children. But God never loses sight of who we are. He alone knows and provides the real answers to the questions "Who am I?" and "Why am I here?"

What do we see when we look in the mirror? Do we see someone who is worthy of love and has value, or do we see a hot mess beyond redemption? Do we choose to see ourselves as beautifully, fearfully, and wonderfully made, as having worth and being valued by the God who made us in his image and likeness? Do we accept God's love for us? Or are we stuck in our insecurities and past mistakes? One thing I know: God never gets stuck in our messes.

PREPARING FOR THE END

As our lives continued to unfold, my deepest, darkest fear was the answer to the question "Who am I without Courtney?" The world did not see our daughter as I did. Most saw the disability and the burden. I saw the laughter, the joy, the sassy attitude, and the gift of her life. As Courtney got older, she still required the same care a baby does. Frequent diaper changes and G-tube feedings were just par for the course. There was suctioning to be done as her ability to swallow deteriorated. These were not easy things, but they were necessary for her care. I did them as best I could. (Don't get me started on my ninja techniques for changing an adult diaper while Courtney remained in her wheelchair!)

Our daughter had fought hard to remain with us, and the rest of our family had made sure she would not be set aside. We took her everywhere. Courtney went to Mass on Sunday, to the movies (especially when there was singing), to museums, and to the mall. Dressing her like a typical teenager drew compliments. It might seem silly, but it was important that she was always dressed neatly and that her wheelchair was spotless. I wanted the world to know that Courtney was loved and well cared for because she had value and worth, even if she could not do what a typical young woman could do.

The flip side was that I had spent so much time making sure that the world saw our daughter's dignity and value that I had forgotten about my own. While Courtney was dressed like royalty, I wore sweats. I wanted her to be seen, but I also hoped that I could just melt into the background of her life.

In the summer of 2014, during Courtney's final visit to the ER, the reality of what was coming became very clear to Jerry and me. Our girl was tired. Her organs were shutting down. Her seizures were out of control. She had fought the good fight for more than two decades, and the doctors were astounded she had made it this far. We had come to the irrefutable conclusion that there were no more treatments or medications to be had. It was time to face what we had known was coming since Courtney lost her sight, the choice that no parent ever wants to make: whether our daughter would die at home or at a hospice facility. The choice itself was easy to make—we had no hesitation in expressing our desire to bring her home, and so we did.

Time was short; the medical team hastened to explain what would happen and how they thought her last weeks would play out. I took it in with a grain of salt since our daughter had outlived all of their previous predictions. Only God had the answers to the how, when, and where of Courtney's death. My job was to continue to care for her and love her home to heaven.

SUSTAINING LOVE

For twenty-two years, I had been Courtney's manager, chief fundraiser, and cheerleader. I had been her advocate, her protector, and her hands and feet out in the world. I made sure she was seen and acknowledged wherever we were. I never allowed anyone to ignore her. I identified so strongly with what I did for Courtney that I had no idea who I was anymore. And now I was going to lose my job. I couldn't stop and think about it because there was too much to be done. Besides, the whole thing frightened me.

Through my blog and social media outlets, I shared openly about the mountain we were getting ready to climb with Courtney. During the previous several years, I had shared our daily life together online, bringing people into our home through technology. Through my words, I allowed others to experience what it was like to love and care for a medically fragile and disabled child. Tens of thousands of people had come to love Courtney as a member of their own families. I knew that our family would need their support.

Courtney's needs were changing by the week, and Jerry and I were a bit overwhelmed trying to stay ahead of what we needed to do for her. There was a new medicine schedule and a new formula for her tube feeds. There was a new mattress to purchase to prevent her from getting bedsores. She was losing weight so fast that none of her clothing fit her.

We had been on the receiving end of tremendous generosity seven years prior when friends led a fundraising effort to pay off the second mortgage on our home so we wouldn't go into foreclosure due to the heavy financial burden that Courtney's care had placed on our family. There were so many emails coming in from people wanting to help that I finally said yes to their kindness once again and made our needs known to our virtual community.

Soon, what we like to call "love bombs" began to arrive at the house. Bob, the UPS guy, came to our door on the very first delivery day to ask if our credit card had been stolen. Jerry looked out front and saw a mountain of boxes. Bob came twice a day for a week; we became very close with him those last few months of Courtney's life. The mailman also shook his head the first day he delivered a pile of boxes to our door.

People were over the top in caring for us the best way they knew how. The online community I had built over the previous seven years rose up in an overwhelmingly wonderful tidal wave of love. They sent clothing for Courtney, meals for the family, assistance with upcoming funeral expenses, and other practical help. It was amazing to watch that love unfold, and Jerry and I were grateful for everything. It took a huge burden off our shoulders as we entered that last valley of sorrow.

NO LONGER NEEDED

One afternoon, I unpacked some new pajamas sent to Courtney from a blog reader in Spain. Breaking down the shipping box the pajamas came in, I had the thought that one day soon I would be broken down and tossed aside just like that box, for the day was coming when Courtney would no longer need me. With that stark realization, I sat down and wept.

What the hell was I going to do without her? I did not have a clue, and it scared the pants off me. I walked around in a daze trying to take in the enormity of losing Courtney. Who was I without her? Protecting and caring for Courtney had been worth the sacrifice and the pain over the course of the previous twenty-two years. I feared, though, that I was not worth that same sacrifice.

When I expressed my feelings to Jerry, he was stunned. "How can you say that?" he asked incredulously. "Are you saying your only purpose in life was to take care of Courtney and now you're done? That's insane. Your life is bigger than that. Courtney is only part of it."

Still, I could not see any purpose to my life without Courtney in it. My sense of identity was so warped that I couldn't fathom my own self-worth. I was so wrapped up in caring for Courtney that I could not see my own future. I was not able to see that I had my own value and purpose separate from Courtney or that God could love me for myself and not just as my daughter's caretaker. I had fallen into the belief that being her caretaker partly made up for all the bad things I had done in my life. For two decades, I had counted on my role of fulfilling Courtney's many needs to provide balance, to keep me on track. How would I carry on without her? I was terrified.

READY TO SAY GOODBYE

During those final months, a steady stream of people came to the house to say goodbye to Courtney and ask for her prayers. It was exhausting. I felt obliged to be there for all these people in addition to taking care of Courtney. Some days their visits felt like an intrusion; other days, they were a welcome distraction. Looking back, I see that this was Courtney's final task—to bring people closer to God one last time as they came to share their prayers with her and love her one final time.

Two weeks before Christmas, my prayer group showed up on our doorstep to serenade Courtney with Christmas carols. These women, whom I had prayed with weekly for more than a decade, wanted to do something they knew would make our girl smile. So I wrapped Courtney up in her warmest blankets and sat with her in my lap on the front porch rocking chair while they sang their hearts out. Courtney beamed as she hummed along with them.

The evening didn't end with the serenade: I invited the women in for hot chocolate and cookies. I settled Courtney into her hospital bed, and each woman made her way into Courtney's room to sit with her, pray over her, and ask for her intercession. At one point, there was an actual line of women waiting outside her door to say their goodbyes to our daughter because she had inspired them to live their faith more deeply.

Courtney had that gift. She moved people to pray, to give of themselves, and to live with a little more empathy and love without judgment—and she did all of this without ever saying a single word. To this day just thinking about that night makes me smile.

At the time, I could not imagine one day without this child in my life or even imagine how I would survive the loss. I wasn't ready to say goodbye to our daughter. What would my days look like without the constant demands that were part of caring for her? I could not believe that life without her would be meaningful. I hung on, not only to Courtney but also to who I was with Courtney.

I began to recognize that I had never truly formed my own identity as an adult woman. First I was Jerry's wife, then I was Jonathan's mom, then I was Courtney and Jonathan's mom, and then I was a full-time caretaker and advocate for a severely disabled child. I was sure that when she was gone I would be obsolete and no longer necessary. Like that used shipping box.

EVERYTHING FOR LOVE

My fears and doubts about my own worth were laid open during this time. They showed a brokenness that had not yet been healed, another one I could not solve on my own. Love is a daily act of the will. I had to choose to see myself as God saw me and strive to acknowledge my worth in his eyes. It is still something I am working through. Although I was willing to make sacrifice after sacrifice for Courtney, I didn't feel worthy of Jesus' sacrifice on the Cross. I just couldn't fathom that God had done all that for me.

It can be extremely difficult to move on, even from something that has been overwhelmingly hard to bear. But in the midst of my fear and confusion, God taught me to find my identity in him and showed our family that we could never lose the gift of Courtney's life. The book you are reading right now is a prime example of the impact Courtney continues to have on the world. God also reassured me that he still had a plan for the rest of our lives, one that stretched beyond what we had been living for the past twenty-two years.

God had made me in his image and likeness, just as he had made Courtney. As I had done everything for Courtney out of love, God had done, and would always do, everything for me out of love. God loved me not for what I did or could do but for who I am.

Where do you find your identity? How tightly are you holding on to the pain and suffering in your life? Are you able to let God re-envision your life apart from it? You are his beloved. He loves you for who you are and has a purpose for your life.

1 PETER 2:9

But you are "a chosen race, a royal priesthood, a holy nation, a people of his own, so that you may announce the praises" of him who called you out of darkness into his wonderful light.

CHAPTER TEN

Everybody's afraid of something. Fear can motivate us to fight, stop us in our tracks, or make us run away. If we allow it to, fear can control every aspect of our lives. The bottom line is that, again, we have a choice to make. We can surrender *to* fear, or we can surrender the fear itself.

Our faith teaches us that if we surrender our fears to God, we can begin to find hope and peace. That surrender is easier said than done. Many of us are living in fear of something we know will cause us pain. And very many of us have allowed this fear to infiltrate every aspect of our lives, stealing our peace and our joy. We eat, sleep, and breathe fear. Yet we still don't want to surrender that fear to God because we are unsure of his love for us. Why? Because we don't truly believe that God is who he says he is—a loving and eternal Father.

Sometimes we think that God is too distant or impersonal to really understand what we're going through, so we decide we can handle things better on our own. Or maybe we are just too ashamed to admit that we can't do it on our own and too proud and stubborn to ask for help.

It is hard to stop fighting and surrender everything to God, even when we know that it is for the best. We still want to be in control and have God solve things our way. We are afraid that if we surrender to God, he is going to lead us down a path we don't like, don't understand, or don't feel confident we can take to complete the journey. But what we forget is that we are never on that journey alone; God is always with us. And God is a much better companion than our fears.

WE BELONG TO GOD

My daughter had one final lesson to teach me about acceptance and surrender: our lives are truly not our own. We belong to God, and in his time he will bring us home. I was going to surrender my most precious daughter whether I wanted to or not. For most of her life, I had been afraid that Courtney would die, but I didn't want her to suffer in this life any more than she already had. Nevertheless, I was terrified of what her absence might mean for the rest of us. The reality of losing our daughter's physical presence forced me to come to terms with the fact that I would need to rely on other people to care for me just as Courtney had relied on me to care for her.

On December 27, 2014, at 1:51 in the morning, our daughter Courtney Elizabeth Lenaburg took her last breath cradled in my arms. Her death broke my heart and saved my soul all at once. Ever faithful, God had honored our request to be with her when she went home to him. With that one last breath, I knew that I would never hold her again, hear her laughter, or see those big, beautiful blue eyes. With that same breath, I believed without a doubt that when Courtney closed her eyes here on earth, she opened them in heaven. After so many years of blindness, the first person she would see would be her Beloved Lord, for whom she had suffered so beautifully. She would stand tall and run into his open arms. I just wish I could have been there to see it with my own eyes.

REELING

Our dear friend Dr. B. was the first phone call we made. He had been there for us and with us as we organized our daughter's hospice care during her last three months. He had walked us through the medical part of what her physical passing would look like, which prevented me from panicking during those last few hours. I wanted to be calm and present for my daughter, and because of his counsel, I was.

When he arrived at our home, he hugged Jerry and me, expressed his deepest sympathies, and then went straight to Courtney's bedside. His care and respect for my child in that moment were beautiful. He had seen, known, and loved my daughter just as she was. The blessing of his presence in the darkest moment of our lives remains a gift in our collective memories of that day. God showed up and spoke through Dr. B.'s calm words and peaceful presence. We would not walk this path alone.

With the arrival of the paramedics and police, we recognized the finality of Courtney's death. We had moved beyond a private passing surrounded by love to the cold realities of process. Official pronouncements were made and the funeral home called. Paperwork was signed, and the waiting began.

My mother stayed with Jonathan in another room. When I told him Courtney was gone, all I saw in his face was pain. He could not bring himself to see her so quiet and still, and we were not going to force the issue. He was overwhelmed with grief and reeling from the emotion of it all. Taking in his pain, I felt like a wine glass shattered into smithereens on the floor. There was no glue strong enough to piece me, or my family, back together.

My biggest fear had come to pass. Courtney was dead. She had gone somewhere I could not go with her. For the first time in twenty-two years, she did not need me, and I didn't know what to do. Nothing would ever be the same. I held her body in my arms and rocked back and forth, quietly weeping and begging God to restore her to life.

I was overwhelmed by the depth of my sadness. I could not do this; I could not live without her. I wasn't smart enough or brave enough or strong enough. Caring for Courtney had made me all of those things, and now she was gone forever. *What the hell was I going to do?*

FULL CIRCLE

The team from the funeral home finally arrived. Jerry lovingly took our daughter from my arms and placed her on the gurney. Watching him gently stretch out her legs, I was transported back in time to the day of her birth. Courtney was a long string bean, and the delivery nurse had needed assistance in order to get a correct measurement of her length. I remembered watching Jerry gently stretch out her legs as she lay in the incubator. Looking down at his sweet newborn daughter, he had had tears in his eyes then. Those tears had returned.

In that moment, I knew that God was there, bringing Courtney's life full circle. It was the first glimmer of grace, but she was so still and quiet. Jerry pulled the sheet up to her chin as though he was tucking her into bed. I begged him to give her back to me, but he stood firm and instead gently held me, whispering his love and concern into my ear.

Jerry walked out to the hearse beside Courtney. There he tenderly kissed our beautiful daughter and covered her face. Not able to bear the weight of it, I fell to the ground and wept. I had no idea how I would get up again. Our daughter had left our home for the last time. Jerry helped me back inside, and I crawled into Courtney's bed, holding her pillow close. It was still warm. It was as if time stopped. I could not imagine ever leaving that bed. Not for anyone or anything.

MISSION POSSIBLE

Overflowing love is what made it possible for me to rise. Over the course of the next few days, God cared for our every need. Funeral costs were paid by anonymous donors. Food appeared out of nowhere. And someone was with us at every step, walking us through the wake, funeral Mass, and burial. God was present in every act of service and kindness to our family. All he asked of us was to receive that kindness in his name.

There were moments of levity amid the tears. My favorite took place the morning of the wake. Jerry and I had gone to the funeral home to see our daughter one last time before she was transported to the church. As I approached Courtney's open casket, I was immediately struck by her hairstyle. In life, my daughter had had a head of riotously curly blonde hair. Think Shirley Temple curls on speed. But the funeral home had straightened her hair! I didn't know what to do or what the protocol was.

It took about thirty seconds before this mama got to work. I told Jerry to watch the door to make sure we were not interrupted. He stared at me, unsure of what crazy plan I had in mind, then quietly began humming the theme from *Mission Impossible*. I leaned into her casket and began Operation Redeem the Curls. Rolling sections of her hair tightly around my fingers, I worked my way around the front of Courtney's face and finally got two or three curls to stay. Jerry sounded the alarm, and I quickly composed myself before the funeral director reentered the room.

As we walked back to the car, Jerry and I laughed for the first time in weeks. We imagined what Courtney would think about the whole curly debacle and how delighted she would be that we were laughing again.

SACRIFICE OF PRAISE

We asked our pastor, Fr. B., to let us have Courtney's wake and overnight vigil in the church the day before her funeral Mass. During the prayer service and the vigil that followed, a steady stream of people came by to share stories, pay their respects, and pray with us and for us. Many of them had never met our daughter in person. We were truly blessed by people's stories of how Courtney had inspired them and their families.

The funeral Mass the next day was a full house. Eight priests, some of whom had heard Courtney's story through social media or their brother priests, concelebrated the Mass. We walked our daughter's casket out of the church as hundreds of people sang Michael Perry's hymn "O God Beyond All Praising." The final stanza wrecked me, but it also gave me strength to keep walking:

> And whether our tomorrows
> be filled with good or ill,
> we'll triumph through our sorrows
> and rise to bless you still:
> to marvel at your beauty
> and glory in your ways,
> and make a joyful duty
> our sacrifice of praise.

Standing by Courtney's grave, I felt that sacrifice of praise come pouring from my heart. I finally surrendered all the pieces of my broken heart to God, the One who had promised he would never leave me. While tracing her name, engraved into the wood of her casket by a Benedictine monk in Iowa, I surrendered my future to the God who said there was still so much more life to live. I surrendered my past, knowing that Jerry and I had done everything we could to love our daughter and care for her as God had asked of us. Jerry, Jonathan, and I walked away, hand in hand, across the broken earth toward an uncertain future knowing only one thing—God is God, and we are not. He saw the road ahead, and we could trust that he would light the way.

LOVE CHANGES THINGS

Death often brings life into perspective, proving the lesson that love is all that matters. It doesn't matter how much money you have or where you live; what matters is how you love. When you love, you can experience even life's deepest losses as overflowing with grace.

When we lost our daughter, God proved that he would never abandon us, not even on our darkest day. He showed up in Dr. B., the eight priests on the altar for her funeral Mass, and a church filled with people, many of whom had their own stories about Courtney. And he showed up in the people who stopped by with a meal or just to spend some time with us in the weeks immediately following. These visits became a basis for ongoing gratitude for God's presence with us.

Even more, I learned that God never takes away what he gives us. The day I surrendered Courtney into God's hands was the day I was able to fully accept the gift she had been and the grace she had brought to our lives.

Courtney came into this world for a purpose. She taught me about love, trust, and surrender to God's will, fully and completely. She truly changed me, and everyone she met, for the better. She left a handprint on our hearts. Though she could not speak, she gave powerful testimony to the joy and grace of our loving God. Courtney proved God's existence to me in a way that no one else has. Because I know that God is real, I am no longer afraid to die. I strive for holiness every day. Although I fail, I just keep trying and trusting in a plan that is greater and grander than anything I could ever devise.

You see, my friend, love changes things. As one of my favorite Christian writers, Bob Goff, says, "Love never leaves you where he meets you." I was no longer the young, twenty-five-year-old woman terrified of God's judgment. Although I had no idea what else he would ask of me, I did know that God is good, no matter what. God wrote Courtney's story, and he continues to write yours and mine. I still had work to do.

LET GO

What is your worst fear? What are you afraid to let go of? It is possible to stop being a slave to fear and set yourself free, my friend. God will never ask for more than he knows you can give with his grace—maybe more than *you think* you can give, but not more than *he knows* you can give. This is where trust comes in.

When you practice trusting God with the small things, it's much easier to trust him when the big things come along. Is there something you are afraid to lose if you place it in God's hands? I have struggled with this question too many times to count. I have had to remind myself again and again that everything I have is a gift given by my Creator. There is no reason to be hesitant to place those gifts back in his hands and trust him with their care. That includes my husband and children. God took my fear and worry and turned them into joy and peace. He can do the same for you.

ISAIAH 41:10

Do not fear: I am with you,
　do not be anxious; I am your God.
I will strengthen you, I will help you,
　I will uphold you with my victorious
　right hand.

CHAPTER ELEVEN

FORWARD WITH GRACE

We all end up grieving the loss of someone close to us: grand-parents, parents, a spouse, siblings, or even a child. When that happens, it's important to recognize that grief has no schedule.

But grief isn't something we experience only with death. We can also experience grief with the loss of a job, a friendship, a home, or a dream. What makes grief so difficult for us to deal with is that it doesn't really end. Loss of any kind creates an ongoing sense that there's something—or someone—missing.

Over time, however, we do regain our balance and begin a process that will hopefully bring us a measure of peace. It's like turning the thermostat down and wearing a sweater inside. At first, you're aware of the cold. But as you adjust to the change, you stop noticing it. You may not be completely comfortable, but the original discomfort is no longer there. Make no mistake: grief never truly goes away. As C. S. Lewis wrote in *A Grief Observed*, "In grief nothing 'stays put.' One keeps on emerging from a phase, but it always recurs."

Lewis understood what he called the "phases" of grief—how you move from shock and denial to acceptance and hope without even realizing you boarded the train. When you're living your daily life in times of turmoil, you're so focused on the pain that you don't perceive that your heart is healing. Until one day, you look back and realize that for the past few weeks you've been getting out of bed without hitting the snooze button six times. You notice that you didn't cry when you opened the dresser drawer and found your late daughter's socks. Or that on your way to work you were no longer thinking about how you'd rather have the flu than get up and go to that job. (Flu or job? Tough choice, right?) Over time—and without your noticing it—your grief recedes and hope slowly reappears on the horizon.

THROUGH THE FOG

How do people navigate through grief? How do we integrate the death of a loved one into the story of our own lives? How do we manage the after-death kinds of problems such as insurance, medical debt, funeral expenses, broken relationships, hurt feelings, reestablishing a family dynamic, and the concern of friends and strangers without wanting to withdraw from the world? With a whole lot of patience, faith, and chocolate chip cookies.

I spent the first six months after Courtney's death walking through the fog of intense pain. I was physically exhausted and emotionally spent. I had a hard time controlling my emotions and was uncertain of how to move forward. Jerry and I both struggled to come to terms with the fact that our daughter was truly gone. I had a hard time sleeping without the sound of Courtney snoring in the baby monitor we kept by our bed. One morning a few weeks after she died, I woke up to what sounded like crying. I ran downstairs to find Jerry standing by Courtney's empty bed, her morning medicines in his hand, weeping.

Grief wasn't the only cause of my emotional turmoil. Due to government cutbacks, Jerry's job was in danger, and we had a mountain of debt to pay off. Although it had been a few years since I had worked outside the home, I knew it was time for me to find employment again. My previous job? Substitute teacher at a school for kids like Courtney. That was not where I needed to be at the time.

A NEW ADVENTURE

The problem was that I had little office experience, a limited education, and no idea what I should do. Otherwise, my prospects were great. In a curious turn of events that can be explained only by God, I wound up interviewing for a job at my home parish. I had not felt very brave since Courtney's passing, but by the end of the interview, I knew without a doubt that a new adventure lay ahead for me—liturgy coordinator. My new job duties encompassed coordinating the liturgical volunteers, caring for the sacred spaces, and scheduling and planning funerals and special liturgies.

It didn't take long before I was surrounded with candle order forms, a map of the sanctuary filled with notes for upcoming Christmas and Easter liturgies, and Prayers of the Faithful to edit for the coming Sunday Masses. I could just imagine what my eighth-grade teacher, Sr. Vincent de Paul, would have said about Mary Beth Green—aka Grade-School Detention Queen—becoming the new Church Lady. I could hear the nuns laughing all the way from their Maryland convent!

Parish ministry gave me a whole new skill set. The Roman Missal became my friend. I also learned how to be the Martha Stewart of St. Mary of Sorrows. Need to remove candle wax from the church carpet? A hot iron and a brown paper bag are the necessary tools. What dish detergent works best to clean the sacred vessels in between Sunday Masses? Palmolive for the win! I became quite adept at ordering hosts from the convent in New

Hampshire and incense from the monks in New York. There were intense discussions about whether to use two-inch-diameter beeswax candles or three-and-a-half-inch. And if you know what's good for you, don't get me started on floral budgets or color schemes for major liturgical events. Who knew there were so many details? For the first time in my life, I truly embraced living the liturgical year.

NEEDED

My favorite part of the job turned out to be working with families to plan their loved ones' funerals. From choosing the readings to gently explaining that there would be no releasing of doves inside the church (true story), I loved every detail. I understood the process because I had been through it myself. By the grace of God, I was able to offer empathy without being overwhelmed by my own grief. My office was a safe zone where tears and shared memories flowed without judgment. It felt good to be needed again, especially as the first anniversary of Courtney's death approached.

When that day finally arrived, there was peace among the tears. I realized that the fog of grief had lifted and life had moved forward. Having to learn new skills on a weekly basis stretched me in ways I'd never experienced before. The job also kept my perfectionist tendencies in check. Each day, I had to determine my priorities and choose what I could actually accomplish from among the many things that needed to be done.

Above all, this new life, with its combination of sadness and hope, required that I up my prayer game. In order to bring God's grace to others, I realized, I needed to spend time in adoration and go to sacramental Confession more frequently. Being around for daily Mass helped as well.

WITH JOY

Before Courtney's death, my daily prayer had been "Lord, let my daughter live another day." Afterward, my daily prayer became, "Lord, allow me to honor you this day and be the face of Christ to someone in need." It was scary to step out of the comfort zone of homemaking and caregiving, but I just kept telling myself, "One step at a time, Mary." I can do anything one step at a time.

Courtney had taught me patience, perseverance, fortitude, faith, and courage. Courtney had taught me to be brave in the scared and to believe in the impossible. Courtney had taught me how to serve with joy. So I kept my daughter's smiling face in my mind's eye as I reached out to those God put in my path.

GOD PROVIDES

Even a year after Courtney's death, Jerry and I were still surrounded by generous people. It was humbling for us to have so many assist us with our medical debt. We knew we'd have to save for Courtney's gravestone for quite some time, and we were okay with that. As usual, God had a different plan. On the first Mother's Day after Courtney's death, a check arrived for the entire cost of the stone. Friends of ours had put out the word that the cost was not something we could manage at the time, and random people had stepped forward once again with generosity and kindness. Every week, people shared stories of how Courtney had impacted their lives. She had gone home to God, but her legacy of love and joy continued to inspire others.

Jerry found a new job, and our family life continued to improve. Despite the lingering challenges, we had seen enough light to understand that hope was an option we could choose. We had found the key to our grief closet, and it was now time to unlock the rest of our lives.

What losses are you grieving? What hardships keep you from hope? I challenge you to examine your life once a day and try to see things differently. It takes time, but grief, for all its bluster and bullying, backs down at the first light of hope.

Do you have something you carry on a daily basis? Maybe it's caring for an aging parent or dealing with a difficult family or work situation. Perhaps it's even the loss of someone you love. There will come a point in your journey when you'll notice a sunset, a blooming rose, or a child's laughter. It is at this point— the point where grief is beginning to back down—that you have a decision to make: you can keep carrying the hurt and pain of loss, or you can put down the burden of loss, choose hope, and move forward with grace.

PSALM 48:15

This is God,
our God for ever and ever.
He will lead us until death.

CHAPTER TWELVE

CHOOSE JOY

Happiness and joy are not the same thing. Happiness is external, based on situations, events, people, places, things, and thoughts. But happiness is also dependent—dependent on external situations, people, or events that align with our expectations. Joy, on the other hand, is internal and, therefore, independent. Joy is independent of changing emotions, circumstances, or external forces. It has nothing to do with people, places, or things. Joy depends only on your ability to choose it no matter what is happening around you. Joy can be found in difficult situations, while happiness cannot.

There is a constant tension between joy and happiness. This tug-of-war is a recurring theme in life and invites us to choose how we will respond to whatever comes our way. Will we choose temporary happiness or lasting and sustaining joy?

THE HOLY SPIRIT

Joy can bring power to your life no matter what difficulties you're facing. When you choose joy, you cooperate with the Holy Spirit, the Superhero of Encouragement. He stands at your side, ready to take on every foe. He empowers you and fills you with the grace you need. No one has your back (or soul) like the Holy Spirit.

Our reliance on the Holy Spirit makes possible what feels impossible. He infuses our very souls with an abundance of trust that all shall be well no matter what storm is brewing in our lives. And more, the Holy Spirit renews us whenever doubt and fear creep into our hearts, whenever we reach for temporal happiness.

We are broken. Life breaks us. Over the years, our struggles reveal our weaknesses and woundedness to the world, leaving us exposed. We may be fearful that we will never measure up or be accepted for who we truly are. We may feel forgotten and set aside. Loss and loneliness may consume us even as we are doing our best to live out our vocation. It's the Holy Spirit that gives us strength to stand in the face of the darkness. Joy is what that strength is called.

NEW STEPS

After Courtney's death, I struggled to make my way through grief and the deep sadness that lingered in my heart. I missed my life with Courtney, but I found happiness and fulfillment in being the parish's Church Lady. As time passed, though, that happiness began to fade, and the emptiness in my heart grew to overwhelm me once again. I became increasingly restless and embarked on some deep soul diving, trying to figure out what God had in mind.

A dear friend, Heather, invited me to speak at a women's conference about God's redemption in my life. It was August of 2016, and Courtney had been gone almost two years. I was terrified at the prospect. But after I took the request to prayer, I accepted the invitation because I felt the Holy Spirit give me a little push.

I soon found myself in Portland, Oregon, on a semi-silent retreat preparing to give my talk. For the three days leading up to the conference, the Holy Spirit and I spent some quality time together in the quiet convent of the Franciscan Sisters of Our Lady of Sorrows. He had spent the last year leading me out of heavy grief and into a new dance, demonstrating each new move with patience and grace, allowing me time to adjust to life's new choreography.

Courtney had been with me in every moment of these spiritual "dance lessons." I felt led to ask God the Father to speak to my heart, peel back my fear, and show me where he wanted me to be and what he wanted me to do. I asked Courtney to intercede for me—that I would hear God speak, if he chose to do so, and that I would listen to him. (Note to self: be ready when asking Courtney to intercede for you. My girl does not play around!)

Oh, did God speak. God was about to give me a new directive that I could not ignore.

LEGACY OF LOVE

When it came to living in the moment, our daughter was the bomb-dot-com. When she woke up in the morning, I never knew how the day would go. Would it be a bad seizure day? Would an infection or illness show up without warning? Or would she suddenly decide she hated peas? I just never knew. Situations would turn on a dime, but she still smiled and laughed and allowed us to love her with wild abandon. We loved her as we wished to be loved ourselves. Her legacy of loving has been her lasting gift to us.

Courtney taught me many things while she was on this side of heaven:

Life is short. Time is precious.
Love fully, and hold nothing back.
Have no regrets.

Live every day as if it's your last one, because it just might be.
Choose joy! Always!

God brought all of this to mind during my retreat. He reminded me that he still had work for me to do. I kept bringing my heart before the Lord, asking him to give me peace and clarity so I would know with certainty that whatever came was from him.

The night before the conference, God spoke. I stood on the stage in front of 250 empty chairs, extremely nervous and very unsure that giving a talk was what God was asking of me. I forgot the opening of my talk and imagined myself falling off the stage in the middle of it. My entire body was shaking, and I wanted to vomit. This was far from what I thought my future would hold. It was terrifying. I stretched out my hands, closed my eyes, and began to pray.

After a few minutes, I opened my eyes and took a few deep breaths. I felt the same as I had in the waters of Lourdes: unsteady and a little confused but convinced that something powerful was happening—a moment of turning and of something new. I slept well that night for the first time in almost two years. I had a profound sense of peace. My heart was brimming with gratitude and joy.

ALL THINGS NEW

The next morning, inspired by my encounter with the Holy Spirit the night before, I put down my talk notes and spoke straight from the heart for fifty minutes about how God had made all things new in my life. I spoke about my husband, son, and daughter—our ups and downs, our failures and triumphs. I shared the story honestly, exposing the bruises and broken parts of my life without fear. Most of all, I told those beautiful women about the Lord's love for them and about his wish to heal them if only they would open the door to their hearts.

There were tears and laughter, both mine and theirs. There were hugs and whispered secrets, prayers asked for and given, and abundant blessings. I was blown away that so many women followed the prompting of the Holy Spirit and headed to Confession. The Holy Spirit showed up in spades, and I was a witness to the wonder of his overflowing grace.

When I went to bed that night, I knew what new challenge God was calling me to. I knew that it was time to step out in faith in his providence for me and my family, to jump off the cliff trusting him with my landing. He was asking me once more to be brave in the scared. I returned home filled with peace and a little bit of excitement.

STEP INTO THE GIFT

Jerry and I prayed about it for a few days and, with a little heavenly prompting, decided it was time to make some changes. In October 2016, after a year of serving my local parish family as liturgy coordinator/Church Lady, I resigned in order to answer the call God placed in my heart to speak and write about his redeeming love. Since then, I've given numerous retreats and talks. I've told my story to encourage others to let go of shame, accept whatever cross God gives, find joy after devastating loss, and let God be sovereign in their lives. I know from personal experience that when you keep your eyes on him, you will never lose hope, no matter what comes your way—and I know what happens when you take your eyes off him. I am living proof of what God can and will do when you learn to trust him.

God gave me an awesome gift. He allowed me to step out of grief and into service, and he showed me that I am capable of doing more than I ever thought I could.

Every time my stomach roils or I break into a sweat thinking about how crazy my new life is, I talk to my girl. Courtney has yet to disappoint. She urges me to choose joy and allow God to continue to redeem all the dark and broken places in my life.

Do you believe that it is possible to find joy in suffering and pain? What would you have to change in order to choose joy? Nothing is left unused, my friend. No one is left unaided. God really is good *all* the time. When we choose joy and offer up our daily trials and tribulations, God's mercy is indeed without bounds or limits. He takes our brokenness and uses it for his purposes, allowing us to share just a little bit in the suffering of the Cross. Sharing in God's plan truly does make the unbearable bearable—it even makes it a gift.

ROMANS 5:3-5

Not only that, but we even boast of our afflictions, knowing that affliction produces endurance, and endurance, proven character, and proven character, hope, and hope does not disappoint, because the love of God has been poured out into our hearts through the holy Spirit that has been given to us.

ACKNOWLEDGMENTS

I thank God for his abundant mercy and love. This book came to be through the encouragement of the Holy Spirit and the mercy and forgiveness I found at the foot of the Cross of Jesus Christ. I live my life for him and him alone.

Thanks to my editor, Jaymie Stuart Wolfe. I have no doubt working with me drove you to binge-eat chocolate on more than one occasion. I cannot adequately express my deep gratitude and the respect I have for you and the entire Ave Maria Press team. You told me once that writing this book would bring me freedom. You were absolutely correct, my friend. Freedom is a beautiful thing. Thank you for believing in me.

I would not be here without Jennifer Fulwiler and Hallie Lord. You two are bold, beautiful, and badass women. Your love of God, family, and your sisters in Christ inspires me. Thank you for Edel, karaoke, well-crafted cocktails, and your prayerful support and confidence in my ability to tell a good story and make people laugh.

Jenna Guizar, Beth Davis, Nell O'Leary, and my sisters at Blessed Is She: you were my beginning in public ministry. You walked me through some of my darkest days of grief and encouraged me to keep getting up when I fell to my knees with the weight of it all. Thank you for standing with me and showing me that life could begin again. May God continue to abundantly bless your mission.

Elizabeth Foss, you inspire me to be a better writer and a better human. Thank you for asking me into your ministry and your heart. God continues to bless me through you. To my sisters at Take Up and Read: I thank you for accompanying me, and for elevating my spirit and my writing.

Thank you to Lisa Hendey, Rachel Balducci, Emily Wilson Hussem, Danielle Bean, Megan Hjelmstad, Haley Stewart, Christy Isinger, Jennifer Madiar, Angie Christie, Jennifer Enderlin, Kathleen Gilles Seidel, Marjanna Bogan, Cristina Trinidad, and every woman who inspires and encourages another to listen to the whispers of the Holy Spirit and follow her dream. Thank you for being a part of my journey to publication. Thank you for your prayers and encouragement.

To our home parish of St. Mary of Sorrows: you welcomed us with open arms all those years ago, and you have walked with us and sustained us through good times and bad. To Fr. Greenhalgh, Fr. Barkett, Brian Kissinger, and Mark Stinard, with whom we served in ministry, thank you for all you do to build the kingdom of God.

To my small group—Cathy B., Lynn R., Bridget M., Beth W., Kathy M., Therese R., Maureen S., Kathy M., and Cathy C.: you prayed with me, prayed over me, and never left my (or Courtney's) side for almost two decades. There are not enough words to properly express my gratitude for your faithfulness in prayer and service during that time. I humbly thank you, my friends.

To the Vault—my Edel '15 sisters Heather, Wendy, Cate, and Rahki: from the meme wars to the late-night emergency texts to the hours spent in adoration praying for one another, you each bring such light and love to my life. I am here because you never allowed me to quit. When I fell, you came alongside me and held a sister up, supporting me and bringing me to the finish line. I love you, and I will always be here for you.

To Maria Cunningham: thank you for the prayers and constant support as well as the lattes and laughter. You have walked beside me during some of my darkest moments and remained a steadfast friend. I am humbled and grateful.

Sharon Wray, you are my sister, my teacher, my critique partner, my confidante, and my friend. This book is a reality because you never once gave up on me and constantly pushed me to reach for greatness. Thank you for bringing Danielle and Karen into my life. Cheers to the Fairfax Four now and always. Patrick, Joe, and Ellen Wray, thank you for sharing your awesome wife and mother.

To Kathryn and Scott Whitaker: sometimes God blesses you with a friendship so wonderful that you just have to say, "God bless Texas." Thank you for your friendship and your hospitality. You both stood in the gap for Jerry and me while I wrote this book. Our gratitude is as abundant as queso and beer on a Friday night. Love from Virginia to you and Team Whitaker.

To Mom and Dad; my brothers (and sweet sisters-in-law) Chris (Shelly), Joe (Pam), Tim (Alex), Rich (Jen), Dave (Ruby), and Andy (Nancy); my sister Marianne; and *all* of my nieces and nephews: you have proven time and time again that family will always be there no matter what. Thank you for loving me and mine through the good and the bad.

To Don and Eleanor, Jalanna, and James: you made my Jerry who he is, and I can never thank you enough for that. He's a keeper for sure.

To DQ, Chrissie Lynn, Niccolo, Hannah Bear, Tortellini, and Noahman: you walked with us and loved us as your own. Thank you for being our sheltering tree—protecting us, providing for us, and profoundly affecting the course of our family's life. Thank you for always having your door open, the Scrabble board set, coffee brewing, and hugs ready. I love you more than horseradish mashed potatoes.

To Jonathan and Courtney: I did not always get it right being your mom, but know that I will never stop loving you both to the moon and back.

To my Jerry: Oh, what a journey we have been on! I cannot imagine a day in my life without you in it. Thirty years is not enough for me. May God grant us at least thirty more. I love you, Jerry, more than you will ever know.

To you, my beautiful and faithful readers, who are now holding my words, my heart: May this book bless you, inspire you to be brave in the scared, and encourage you to keep getting up when life pushes you down. May you always know that you are loved beyond measure by a good and mighty God who will never leave you. Thank you for your prayers and support.

MARY E. LENABURG is a full-time author and Catholic speaker who has given keynotes at conferences across the country, including the Edel Gathering, the Diocese of Grand Rapids Women's Conference, Mary's Mantle Breakfast, and at the Northwest Catholic Women's Conference in Oregon. A writer with Take Up and Read, she has contributed to five meditation books. She also has contributed to two other books.

She has appeared on Catholic radio and podcasts, including *The Jennifer Fulwiler Show*, *The Hallie Lord Show*, *Fountains of Carrots*, and *Girlfriends*. Lenaburg serves her home parish in many roles, including as a catechist, sacristan, and extraordinary minister of Holy Communion.

She and her husband, Jerry, live in Fairfax, Virginia, with their son, Jonathan. Their daughter, Courtney, passed away in 2014.

Facebook: marylenaburgwriter
Instagram: @marylenaburg
Pinterest: @Mary Lenaburg
Twitter: @marylenaburg

AVE

AVE MARIA PRESS

Founded in 1865, Ave Maria Press,
a ministry of the Congregation of
Holy Cross, is a Catholic publishing
company that serves the spiritual and
formative needs of the Church and its
schools, institutions, and ministers;
Christian individuals and families; and
others seeking spiritual nourishment.

———◦◉◦———

For a complete listing of titles from

Ave Maria Press

Sorin Books

Forest of Peace

Christian Classics

visit www.avemariapress.com

AVE MARIA PRESS
Notre Dame, IN
A Ministry of the United States Province of Holy Cross